ASSISTING
LEARNING
&
SUPPORTING
TEACHING

ASSISTING LEARNING

& SUPPORTING TEACHING

A Practical Guide
for the Teaching Assistant
in the Classroom

Anne Watkinson

David Fulton Publishers
London

David Fulton Publishers Ltd
Ormond House, 26–27 Boswell Street, London WC1N 3JZ

www.fultonpublishers.co.uk

First published in Great Britain in 2002 by David Fulton Publishers

Note: The right of Anne Watkinson to be identified as the author of this work has been asserted by her in accordance with the Copyright, Designs and Patents Act 1988.

Copyright © Anne Watkinson 2002

British Library Cataloguing in Publication Data
A catalogue record for this book is available from the British Library.

ISBN 1–85346–794–4

Typeset by Elite Typesetting Techniques, Eastleigh, Hampshire
Printed in Great Britain by Bell and Bain Ltd, Glasgow

Contents

This book is dedicated to
Andrea, Eunice and May,
who showed me
what good teaching assistants can do.

Acknowledgements

I would like to thank:

- Professor Barbara MacGilchrist at the London Institute of Education, University of London, whose constant encouragement kept me going and helped me to find out what TAs really do;
- Essex County Council, my employer at the time of my research, for helping my work with teaching assistants, and particularly to my line manager, Fred Corbett, who encouraged me to study in the first place;
- all the teaching assistants and teachers who participated in courses and discussions over the years;
- the head teachers, staff and pupils in the schools I visited, particularly the two study schools: Beehive Lane Community Primary School and Tiptree St Luke's Church of England (Controlled) Primary School, and Tiptree St Luke's Church of England (Controlled) Primary School and William de Ferrers School for the photographs;
- Sage Publications Ltd for permission to reproduce Figure 5.2 on p. 50;
- those who read and commented on the text;
- Jill Foakes for her drawings on which the cartoons are based;
- and my supportive husband, for his endless patience with the phone calls, keeping the house going while I worked, and his maintenance of my ICT system.

Introduction

There are over 127,000 teaching assistants (TAs) in England alone, working in a whole variety of ways with children of all ages and of all abilities. Until recently the role of teaching assistants was as diffuse as it was invisible, partly because of the wide variety of tasks they undertake.

They used to be seen as an extra pair of hands to wash paint pots and care for grazed knees, then as a useful extra adult to support pupils with special needs. As people realised their potential, and teachers and managers used them more effectively, along with the impact of the Literacy and Numeracy strategies of the late 1990s, they became recognised as an important factor in raising standards. They now help teachers in the crucial areas of teaching and learning. In the past, teaching assistants were often appointed in an informal way, such as when the need arose to support a special pupil, or when a bit of extra funding came the way of the school, but they are now becoming full members of the school staff team.

TAs are also a group with an enormous fund of goodwill, enthusiasm and growing expertise. As their profile has been raised, everyone is more conscious of their role and the need to help the TA do a good job. Partnership and teamwork have become key issues in schools.

The name 'teaching assistant' implies that the TA does some teaching and this still causes problems for many teachers. This book aims to help TAs both to support pupils in their learning and to assist teachers by teaching – yet under the direction of qualified teachers at all times. Teachers carry responsibility for the learning of the pupils in their class, and for this responsibility teachers have long training and different pay scales from TAs.

This book is for TAs who are working in a general capacity in schools, supporting pupils and teachers, and also supporting the curriculum. The first two chapters look at how TAs can get started in the job. Chapters 3, 4 and 5 examine the three aspects of what affects learning in the classroom: the curriculum; the learners (the pupils); and the adults. Looking at how we ourselves learn gives us some idea of how we can support pupils as learners. The book goes on to describe the school context, and then takes a brief look at the local and national elements that support TAs and teachers in their work. Finally, it offers a few ideas on continuing career development for TAs.

It may be possible to read this book as an isolated TA, or even as part of a course, but hopefully you can enlist the help of a friendly teacher, usually called a mentor. You can do this formally, through your line manager or your head teacher, or informally. However, you do need to remember that teachers these days are under considerable pressure to do many things outside their pupil contact hours, and may not feel they have the time to undertake mentoring a TA. But those who have agreed to do it have gained in the long run from having a more informed assistant, one who understands the context of the classrooms and schools in which he or she works.

Chapter 1

Before you start

You may have various reasons for applying for a job as a TA. The research shows you are likely to be a woman and not a recent school leaver. You are possibly a mother and probably have or have had children at school. Somehow you have found the time to go in and help at your children's school. You found you enjoyed working with children, you know a lot about them from having your own, and the school staff have found your help useful. Perhaps the school then advertised a part-time job, or a member of staff approached you, and you found you could get paid for something you are enjoying and which fits in with having the family.

Some of you have recently left school, and think that you may enjoy working with children. In the past, the only possibility of getting qualified to do this was to become a teacher or opt to work with very young children and become a nursery nurse. Many more possibilities are now available and, hopefully, some of you are considering a career as an assistant in a mainstream school – a TA.

Some of you left school several years ago, and want a change of career, and see working with youngsters as more satisfying. That it will be. Some of you may even be among the lucky ones to have found a full-time job although these are still few and far between; most TA jobs are for term time only, and many for pupil contact time only.

Whatever your background before starting the job, you are bringing a wealth of experience, knowledge and understanding with you. You have probably had to fill in an application form and have an interview so you will have met some of the staff before you start, and visited at least part of the school, even if you were not already familiar with it.

Before you start as a new TA, someone in the school should take responsibility for your induction (though unfortunately this isn't always what happens). All schools are different, and even if you have done the job before, there are things you need to know about how you are going to work in this school. Even if you know the school well, being employed will bring changes.

Finding out about the job

You need to know

Your way about (maybe there is a map?)

Where to hang your coat and where the toilet facilities are

What to wear – some schools have a 'dress code' for every day; some lessons such as science need protective clothing, while others like PE need special clothing

Where to go for a refreshment break or lunch

Who to go to for any information about your job

What to do if you are ill on the premises or cannot come to work

What the guidelines are about pupils' and adults' behaviour, and what the pupils are to call you

When you will be given a job description, when it will be reviewed, and how

What other contractual conditions of service there are, like having a probationary period

Who will brief you about child protection and confidentiality

What is expected of you regarding attendance at meetings and going on courses

Who to go to if you need help on a personal problem, or to discuss your work

---

Some of this may seem obvious, but can frequently be overlooked. Assumptions can be made by busy managers that you know all this kind of thing.

You do need to know some of the school's policies, particularly those on Health and Safety, Confidentiality and Child Protection, right from the start. There is more detail about these in Chapter 6. Many schools now have a staff handbook, and some even have one especially for TAs. Handbooks usually contain valuable information about life in the school in general, who does what and when, and who is responsible for each subject, area, and resource that you might need. It will give you names of governors, and titles and locations of policies to which you might want to refer.

Once you have established to whom you go about your job, you can then work with them to find out all the other matters. You will be directly responsible to either a line manager such as the SENCO (the co-ordinator of children with special educational needs), or possibly a deputy head or head teacher. You will be working in a classroom with one or more pupils. You will be working directly with a qualified teacher who is responsible for your work as well as that of all the pupils in the class. Sometimes, indeed, teachers have felt that TAs are an added burden, like an extra pupil. It is up to you to prove them wrong!

You will become a professional, a member of staff, even if you are employed for only five hours a week. This gives you a status with the pupils. You may have worked in the local playgroup before you came to the job, where they called you by your first name, and treated you as an auntie. The pupils in the school will see you differently, and this helps you to be firm about school matters, and yet maintain the friendly approach. Calling pupils by their first names and being called by your family name, with an appropriate title – Mr, Mrs or Miss – establishes your position, particularly if you are near to the pupils in age, or knew them more informally before becoming a TA. This does not mean you are distant or pompous, just professional. Being appropriately friendly, establishing rapport and the foundations for a working relationship with both staff and pupils, are important. The reasons for this will become clearer as you read on.

Becoming a professional

Now you are a professional, you may have to rearrange things at home. Child care before and after school may be needed if you are to talk to teachers out of pupil contact time, and attend meetings and courses. Child care may be needed if your children are ill, although usually senior staff are understanding, so long as you do not take advantage of them.

You may need to rearrange your domestic routines to fit in with the new job. It really helps if partners or family members understand what your new commitments might entail, and if friends understand you are not as free to do the things you may have been used to doing. But be sure to leave time for yourself and your family; you do not want to gain a job but lose something else you value. Being a rounded person with outside activities and responsibilities means you are a more interesting individual to be with the pupils.

Beware of taking on too much. Becoming a midday assistant as well as a teaching assistant may seem to make sense in terms of continuity for the pupils, but it usually means you do not get your lunch until after school. Snacking or omitting meals does not help your body, and a break from work, even for a short time, refreshes your mind.

Be wary of talking about people or pupils you meet in your new job. It is tempting to tell someone about incidents that occur or personal details about people that you learn from conversations, but being a professional means sharing comments of that nature only with your professional colleagues. Confidentiality about school matters is vital. However, you can and should talk about the principles of the job outside the school. Talking always helps you clear your mind, and putting thoughts into words means you have to organise those thoughts. Don't bore your family though!

Being a TA can be emotionally demanding. The circumstances of some pupils may distress you. You will become close to some pupils, particularly if you are to assist one with special needs. As a professional you will need to be more objective than a parent, yet properly caring. This is why it is important to have someone in the school to share your feelings with. All school staff need personal support about their job at some time, so do not be afraid to ask.

Take it one step at a time. In this way you will gain confidence, and knowledge and understanding. Maybe becoming a TA should carry a health warning – beware enthusiasm! Once you start, you will want to learn more, take more courses, become a better TA; you may even want to go on to become a teacher. You do not have to do it all at once. It may be that you need a year or so out of your career as a TA to undertake some family commitment, to care for a sick relative, or because your partner's job or own children's needs become more demanding. Do not worry about it; nothing you do in the job or at home is wasted, it all adds up to the person that is you.

Having a social life, reading novels, listening to music and doing whatever interests you is essential to keeping you a balanced and interesting person. You can then bring to the staffroom or the classroom another dimension or opinion. You may find you want to take artefacts (objects of interest) into school from home, or collect home things to use in school, like photographs or things you find on holiday. It sometimes becomes difficult to separate school life from home life, and this is a balance which you have to find for yourself.

If you are going to study at all at home, even reading a bit here and there, find a space on the shelves for your school things and try to find a time just for you. Some TAs studying for the longer courses end up working after everyone else in the house has gone to bed. This may work for a short time, but it should not become a lifestyle. Do talk these sorts of things over with your family members; they may have ideas to help, and it is good to involve them in your new experiences.

Being professional also means that, even if you are concerned about things at home, once you step over the threshold of the school you give school matters your full attention. Smile, and respond to others. Remember, we all have problems – and putting them aside for a time may even help us cope with them. If it is really difficult, find your line manager and talk it through at a convenient time for you both.

Enjoy the job. Being a TA is a very satisfying career, never dull, and full of opportunity.

Chapter 2

Getting started in the job

Responsibility

Whatever you are asked to do, the responsibility for the teaching and learning of the TA is held by the qualified teacher. The DfEE (Department for Education and Employment, now the DfES, Department for Education and Skills) agreed on the following (TAWG 2001):

> Although Teaching Assistants are not specifically identified in the Teachers' regulations, appropriately trained Teaching Assistants can manage groups from a class without the presence of a teacher, so long as the work they are doing is under the direction and control of the teacher.

Ground rules

Discuss the list of useful ground rules with the teachers with whom you are going to work. You may find that just talking the list through with your mentor or line manager will be enough, but it is wise to check that you don't need to do anything more formal.

Things to remember

Useful ground rules

Before you start in the classroom find out:

Where to go in the room, or whether you are to work outside the room

     If outside, where you go for help and when you are
     to complete your time with the pupils

Whether you can approach the teacher during the lesson

What decisions you can make for yourself

When you can talk things over with the teacher

Where you can find materials to work with

Which pupils you are going to work with and what their particular needs are

What you are to do with them and why – what is the purpose of their task

---

What kind of end product the teacher expects, or is it the doing of the task that is important (or both)

What to do if the pupils misbehave or things go wrong

What to do if they finish what the teacher wanted them to do

Whether you can write in their books or on their worksheets

How the teacher wants to hear about how the pupils did the task

Whether you contribute or question during the teacher's input time

Establish some lines of communication for the future to ensure:

> You understand the needs of the pupils with whom you are to work
>
> You know how to find out what the teacher wants you to do on a regular basis, and what the pupils are expected to learn and achieve in the time you are with them
>
> You know what sorts of things you can do or plan to do on your own initiative

Do not arrive at a classroom after the lesson has started unless you have spoken to the teacher first. You need to establish communication with the teacher of that class before you go there for the first time.

As you get to know your way around the school and the classroom, try hard to remember names. Watch how other members of staff do things, and talk this over with your mentor if you are seeing different practices in different places. You need to establish what the senior management are aiming for, as well as what the individual teachers want.

Duty of care

You have a duty of care whenever you are working with people, but most particuarly when you're working with children. For some of you, this may be your main task. If you are appointed to work with a physically disabled child for a particular task or have a post in a special school as a care assistant, care may be your main duty. If that is the case then you will need specialist guidance and training for the particular skills you need. This book doesn't aim to cover special needs but there are plenty that do. A good place to start is the David Fulton Publishers' individual special needs list: call the publishers for a copy of their catalogue (020 7405 5606) or check their website (www.fultonpublishers.co.uk).

Everyone needs to consider their own personal and professional development whether or not they are in paid employment. All of us have certain documents we need to keep for a lifetime, beginning with a birth certificate. It is very useful to have some sort of record of your education, your experiences, both within and outside work, and somewhere to keep those documents so that you know where they are when life sends you new opportunities.

Keeping a portfolio

You should consider beginning a personal professional development portfolio. This is really just a loose-leaf collection of information and evidence about you. You could start one when you start this job. An example is given in the *Teaching Assistant File* (DfEE 2000a and DfES 2001a), part of their TA induction materials, although this also contains a lot of material about literacy, numeracy and behaviour management which may or may not be useful to you. Start your own portfolio if the school does not have a system – any ringbinder will do. Think of your personal portfolio as a reference collection, and have other files or folders for working documents, such as course notes. You will find a file like this exceptionally useful if you ever have to compile a curriculum vitae (CV), but it's also helpful as a personal touchstone if you ever feel a little low.

A wealth of experiences

A personal portfolio

Have dividers in your ringbinder for:

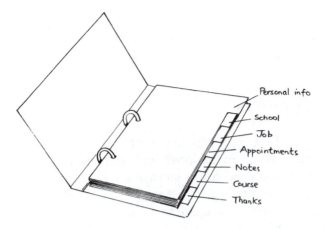

- your personal information and history
- your place of work and relevant documents
- your job and how it is going
- documentation concerning any professional review or appraisals that you may have
- your own notes
- a record of the course details, dates and outcomes of courses, any associated certificates which you want to keep for reference later (if you go on a course, you're likely to need a separate file for the course materials)
- letters of appreciation or references

The thin plastic pockets designed for ringfiles are ideal containers for documents like certificates, but you will need extra wide dividers if you use these.

The personal section

You have a wealth of life experiences regardless of formal qualifications. Don't underestimate these or undervalue yourself.

Most of us change jobs several times in our working lives, and sometimes the change of direction requires experience we have forgotten about. For instance, you may have learnt a language to go on holiday which would be really helpful later. Parenting skills are useful for a TA, as are the organisation skills which you might have developed in connection with social activities – such as being an officer in a sport's club – and your practical 'do-it-yourself' skills. Sewing, potting and painting are practical skills in today's primary schools, and caring skills, first aid experience and organising skills from running things like scouts or guides can be useful whatever age the pupils.

Suggestions for the personal section of your file

After your name, address, telephone number etc., make a note of all those important numbers which you can never find – National Insurance number, hospital number, car registration, telephone number of next of kin and your solicitor, and so on.

Your educational history should include:
  the names of schools and colleges you have been to and dates attended
  what examinations you have taken and what the results were
  any other courses you have taken and what qualifications you have gained, with grades and dates (keep any certificates and diplomas here)

Life experiences – what things you have done other than paid employment (these could include parenting, caring, clubs and societies, craft and domestic achievements, interests and hobbies)

Employment experiences with dates

A record of anything you have produced: a booklet, a craft object, even a child! (you could keep photos of them here)

Anything else that might be relevant that you want to keep a record of:
  holidays/travel experiences
  disasters you coped with
  major events you attended

Where you are working

If you have completed any form of induction you will already have gained some pieces of information about your school. Put these into the school section of your personal portfolio. Some of these will be useful to you when you read Chapter 6. If you get any addresses, policies or other information about the school, here is a useful place to keep it, where you will know where to put your hands on it. The school prospectus may be useful starting point. Chapter 6 on the school context has suggestions of policies which you should know about. You may not need copies of all of them; just a reference or a photocopy of the relevant pages may be enough.

Your job

This section can begin with your job description. You could also include any notes regarding your employment, or comments on your work as a TA from visitors. You might keep photographs of visits or activities with which you have been involved, programmes of school productions, cuttings from the local paper recording events in the school. It is somewhere to keep notes of your own thoughts about your job for future reference if they do not need immediate action. You should also keep a record of any meetings or courses you have been to, adding where you can what use these may have been to you.

The aim is to be able to reflect on your job so that you can improve your personal competence, and maintain your own self-esteem and self-confidence. The rest of the file will become more useful as you progress in your job, but it will be a place where you can keep your notes until their value becomes clearer to you.

Chapter 3

Understanding the curriculum

Before you start in a classroom, you will need to make contact with the class teacher with whom you are going to work. You may be given verbal directions or a written lesson plan to complete some kind of task with the pupils. The task will not be given simply to occupy the pupils but to help them to learn something of value.

What the pupil learns in the classroom is a match made up of three elements:

- what the teacher wants the pupil to learn (usually based on the curriculum);
- the learning style and characteristics of the pupil; and
- the activities of the adults teaching and supporting the learning.

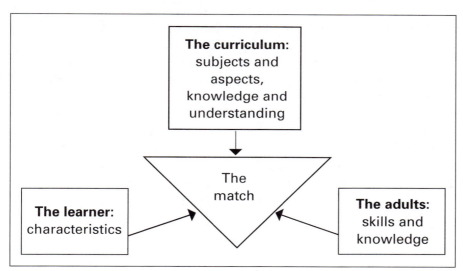

Figure 3.1   The match between the curriculum, the learner and the adults in the classroom

The success of the activity or task depends on an appropriate match of these elements. If any one of these is inappropriate, then something goes wrong. The curriculum can be too hard or easy, the learner can be unhappy or uncomfortable, or the adults may not know the subject well enough or understand what they are supposed

Getting started in the classroom

to be doing. As a teaching assistant, you are not responsible for making the match, but you can assist in all three aspects of the system by understanding more about each.

Another way of looking at what happens in the classroom is to think of it as a cycle (Figure 3.2), with each part leading into the next. Thus:

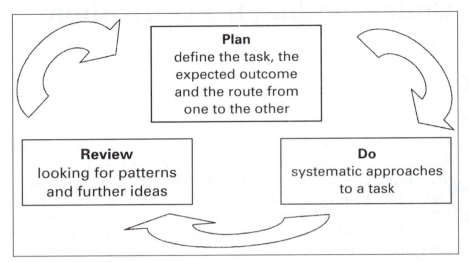

Figure 3.2   The plan, do, review cycle

1. **Plan:** Plan and prepare what you are going to do. This includes knowing more about the topic than the pupil does, and knowing as much as you can about the pupil before you meet.
2. **Do:** 'Deliver' what you have planned. You'll need to adapt it to anything that you didn't (or couldn't) foresee.
3. **Review:** Assess what took place for the pupils and report back to them, or others if necessary. Clear up, and think about what has happened.

Some of you may say: 'But I am only paid for "the doing", the actual time in the classroom, so when can I prepare or feedback?' If this is a problem you must discuss it with your line manager or class teacher as soon as possible. This book is recommending best practice, and best practice includes planning, preparation, feedback and clearing up time. The classroom activity relies on these other items to be most effective.

Planning and preparation

Sometimes the planning seems an unnecessary chore, particularly when you have done it all before and are becoming experienced. But all tasks require planning (even shopping works better if you've made a list) and the better prepared you are, the more smoothly the task will run, and the actual work on the day is minimised. If plans are in writing, then other people can help, or step in at the last minute in a crisis to take over. This holds true for all tasks and activities, including classroom planning.

Teachers have three levels of planning: long term, medium term and short term.

1. **Long term planning**: Teachers have a map of the broad areas of the curriculum they have to cover in the school year. Secondary schools usually convert this to a syllabus with each lesson mapped out for the year, but primary schools, teaching all subject areas, usually allow each class teacher more flexibility to plan their programme. They still have to ensure everything is covered and so often link subjects: for instance, environmental studies may be linked to science and geography; or writing might be about a history topic; and mathematics from the mathematics lesson is practised in technology lessons. Each school will have a policy and a scheme of work for each subject area which the teacher has to follow.

2. **Medium term planning**: Each term teachers plan in greater detail what is to be covered each week. This enables them to arrange relevant visits or visitors, ensure they have the appropriate resources and books, and gives them an opportunity to review the previous term's work. Thus they can build in repetition or revision of topics the pupils are less sure of.

3. **Short term planning**: Weekly, teachers plan in detail, setting down the objectives of what each lesson should achieve in terms of what the pupils will learn. This is where the needs of individual and groups of pupils can be properly addressed. These plans will include what each group is going to do to achieve the objectives, and any other activities such as practical work, assessment activities, and the role of any additional adults in the classroom such as the TA.

As a TA, you too should plan and prepare and, like the teacher, you can think of your own planning in terms of three levels.

Your long term planning

This is about your own professional development. Decide how you are going to prepare yourself for the job and what knowledge you need to acquire, both in your skills development and in the subject matter of the curriculum you are involved with. Are there courses that you might take? What reading might you do and what meetings could you go to? Discuss these matters with your class teacher, mentor or line manager.

It will be part of the planning to know what the pupils should be learning from the lessons you will support. Sources of information are the National Curriculum (NC), the schemes of work published by the Qualifications and Curriculum Authority (QCA), or your school's scheme of work or syllabus. These are reference and planning documents and may be hard going – there's more about them later in this chapter. You will need to refer to the teachers to understand some of the jargon in the text.

Other useful sources of subject information are the various staffroom handbooks. If you have been hearing reading, ask for the handbook that goes with the reading scheme you are using. If you are using computers, find a handbook for the Internet or whatever aspect interests you. Talk to the subject co-ordinator or the head of department; they may have some good books to lend you. Remember, your motivation is important to your learning.

If you are involved with literacy or mathematics lessons you should be part of the school in-house training in these areas, and have access to the relevant strategy materials. You will find some useful additional help in these areas from books by Fox and Aplin (see Further Reading). If you are involved in science lessons, meetings of the local branch of the Association for Science Education (ASE) may be of interest to you; they have special meetings for technicians.

Many local authorities run courses in subject areas for TAs, with or without teachers present, but these may be in the day time, and you will certainly need to book them through the school.

Your medium term planning

You need to know more about the learners you will be involved with, and whether they have particular needs or circumstances which you ought to understand. SEN (Special Educational Needs) is a label given to a pupil who has some needs which, if not dealt with, will hinder learning. There will be an Individual Education Plan (IEP) for these pupils. There are plenty of books on SEN subjects.

SEN designation usually refers to children at the lower end of the ability spectrum, and those with behaviour problems. All pupils have individual needs. One group not always identified by an IEP but who do have particular needs are high ability pupils. They can be emotionally or socially immature for their learning ability and this can lead to behaviour problems caused by frustration. Whatever the case, you should ascertain whether the pupils you have to work with have SEN, and if so what these special needs are, and the appropriate way of dealing with those needs in the opinion of the school. You need to be briefed. If you live in the locality, you may even be able to contribute helpful information about the child's background which is new to the school. As you work with the children, you will get to know them well, just by the amount of small group or one-to-one contact you have with them. So make an arrangement to feed back to the teacher any information you have or obtain, in as appropriate, efficient and confidential manner as possible.

While the class teacher in a primary school will know the children well and be able to brief you on special circumstances or needs, in a secondary school it is the SENCO who tracks the children through the various subject areas and as they go up the school. The SENCO may even be your line manager; he or she will have information on the individual children on the SEN register and will brief you on what you need to know.

Whatever the age of the child or young person in your care, their health and safety must be paramount. Is where you will be working warm and safe? Do you know where to go for help, or what to do in a fire drill? Have you found out what behaviour management strategies are expected of you? Are the chairs and tables and equipment appropriate in the area you will use, and if not can you do anything about it? It is bad practice to find small children kneeling at computers, TAs using scissors that will not cut, adults talking to each other when accompanying a group of children across a road, and poor levels of lighting in the work area. Should there be a real problem, in your opinion, then do something about it as tactfully and politely as possible.

Your short term planning

It should not happen that you arrive in a lesson as it begins (or even after it has started) to be briefed by the teacher as to what to do or to pick up from the pupils what is expected of you. This is 'seat of the pants' working, occasionally necessary in an emergency, but otherwise to be avoided.

The best practice allows paid time for the TA and teacher together outside pupil contact time. In this way a partnership is built up, relationships develop, questions are asked, and possible problems explored before they occur. This need not be long. In a primary school, half an hour a week is sufficient for a TA allocated to one class. It does get difficult where TAs relate to more than one class, and even more difficult in secondary school, where the non-pupil contact time is usually with the SENCO rather than the subject department.

The next best thing is for the teachers to provide the TA with a copy of their short term plans for the lessons where the TA is present, or to draw up special plans for the TA. Either way there needs to be a short induction time for the teacher to explain the layout and jargon used. The most important thing for you, as TA, to know is the *objective* of the lesson, and the part you will play in achieving this. (Different terms are used for the learning objective; it could be teaching objective or proposed learning outcome.) Following this will be some kind of activity or task or process which will take place in the lesson. Some teachers then list the pupils for the TA and their particular needs, and leave a space for the TA to write in any feedback. You then complete this during the lesson, and hand it back at the end, if there is no time for verbal feedback.

Some ideas for planning and recording forms can be found in the *Teaching Assistant File* (DfEE 2000a pp. 9.17–9.19 and DfES 2001a pp. 1.38–1.40). Some schools run a simple exercise book system. This provides a communication opportunity for the teacher and TA, where time is tight.

Whatever the system you must try to get hold of the information *before* the lesson, then you can prepare. Even if you can only prepare mentally, your participation will be that much more effective. But if you are able to collect resources or find different ones, this will bring your participation in the lesson to life. If, for instance, it is a science lesson on light, you may have photographs of an eclipse, or an old telescope, or a rechargeable torch that you can bring in if you know what aspect is to be taught that day. You may want to do some background reading about a country that is to be covered in a geography lesson, or a period in time for a history lesson. You may also need to prepare the area in which you are to work for an art session. You can ensure you have an apron for the messy activities, or proper shoes to go out into the grounds looking for minibeasts (insects, snails, worms and the like). For physical education (PE), you should be appropriately dressed with plimsolls or tracksuit. As well as needing to protect yourself and your clothes, you are a role model to the pupils.

Part of your role may be to prepare materials for the teacher so you will need to find out where things are kept. Do you know how to operate the photocopier, and where the spare paper is kept and how to load it? You may be asked to make audio or video recordings. Again, make sure you know where everything is, how to operate the equipment properly and safely, how to leave it for others to use, and where recorded material is kept and how it is filed. If access to equipment and resources is part of your job, it is worth spending a little of your own time familiarising yourself with operating instructions, resource areas, stock management systems, and who to go to for help.

TAs in secondary schools have been tempted to prepare worksheets for their pupils, in various curriculum areas, to enable them to access the curriculum in that subject. Do check with the teacher concerned before you plan detailed work of this kind for particular children. It needs a great deal of curriculum understanding, pupil understanding, liaison and trust with the teachers.

What is a curriculum?

A curriculum can mean a course of study at a school, but really the word covers everything that goes on in school. The formal part, the prescriptive part that is now written down, is what most people think of when they refer to a school curriculum. But children learn much more than this in school. Probably you remember things you learnt at school that neither the teachers nor your parents knew about – and maybe if they had, they would not have approved. You learnt about other pupils and teachers themselves, about how friendships work, and how to keep out of trouble. These are all part of what is learnt at school. These aspects are sometimes called the informal curriculum or the hidden curriculum. The informal curriculum covers what goes on between lessons: in the corridors or the playground, assembly or clubs; and the hidden curriculum covers the relationships and climate, the way you feel when you work or visit a place.

THE WHOLE CURRICULUM

THE FORMAL CURRICULUM

THE LEGALLY REQUIRED CURRICULUM IN
ENGLAND AND WALES

THE NATIONAL CURRICULUM

THE CORE SUBJECTS
English
Mathematics
Science

Design and technology
Information and
communication technology
History
Geography
Modern foreign languages (secondary)
Art and design
Music
Physical education
Citizenship (secondary 2002)
Welsh (in Wales)

Religious education
Sex education (secondary)
Careers information (secondary)
English and ICT across the curriculum

Additional subjects determined by the school

Includes the informal and hidden curriculum

Figure 3.3   The school curriculum

The formal, informal and hidden curricula

The formal curriculum

This covers what schools aim to teach. If you work in a state school, this includes the NC as a legal requirement in English and Welsh schools. Independent schools are free to set their own curriculum, although some follow the NC or parts of it. The NC is dictated by government, and is an entitlement for all children of statutory school age, five to 16. Parts of it have now been rewritten three times. Scotland has an advisory NC and Northern Ireland has its own version.

The National Curriculum

Making the curriculum a legal requirement means that everyone has a right to be taught certain subjects at certain ages, and it ensures there is a breadth and balance, coherence and consistency, relevance and differentiation. These words are all written into the legal descriptions of the NC. It also has its own terminology: programmes of study, attainment targets, level descriptors, and key stages. All schools will have copies of the documents and it is well worth reading the introductory pages (DfEE 1999a, 1999b pp. 10–13) on 'Values aims and purposes', and what is required of schools and teachers. The latest revision published to begin in September 2000 stated the aims of this NC as:

> Aim 1: The school curriculum should aim to provide opportunities for all pupils to learn and to achieve...

> Aim 2: The school curriculum should aim to promote pupils' spiritual, moral, social and cultural development and prepare all pupils for the opportunities, responsibilities and experiences of life...

> The four main purposes of the National Curriculum: To establish an entitlement, to establish standards, to promote continuity and coherence and to promote public understanding. (DfEE 1999a, 1999b p. 13)

The original documents laid out the subjects of a NC which had to be studied by pupils in England: these were English, mathematics and science, which it denoted as the core subjects; and the foundation subjects of design and technology, information technology (IT), art, music, PE, history and geography and, after age 11, a modern foreign language. Religious education (RE) was included in a basic curriculum, and cross-curricular linked areas were described later. Welsh was made an additional subject for pupils in Wales. It aimed to challenge expectations and raise standards and broaden the range of subjects studied. Spiritual, moral, social and cultural education, citizenship and environmental education are now more closely defined by the new Curriculum 2000.

At first, for some teachers and schools, a nationally imposed curriculum was a burden. Schools and teachers had previously been free to teach what and when they felt appropriate to their school or their pupils. The original documentation looked daunting, with a separate ringfile for each subject. This did not matter so much in secondary schools, where each teacher is usually only responsible for one subject, but primary teachers have to teach all subjects except the modern language.

The National Curriculum overload

Yet even now, with several reviews and considerably more regulations about documentation, and accountability, England's NC is seen across the world as relatively minimal compared with many other countries. We do not have legislation that insists on the same material being delivered in the same way at the same time on each day of the week, each week, month and year. We do not have standardised, centrally legislated and produced lesson texts from which we all work. Some countries do.

You will find the jargon of the NC hard at first, so it will help to understand a few technical terms. **Programmes of study** describe what should be taught, the basis for planning and teaching. There is a framework in a nine level scale for assessment in **attainment targets** (eight levels and a level for exceptional performance) with **level descriptions** for each level. An attainment target sets out the 'knowledge, skills and understanding that pupils of different abilities and maturities are expected to have by the end of each Key Stage' (Education Act 1996). Each level description describes the types and range of performance that pupils working at that level should show. The level descriptions provide the basis for making judgements about pupils' performance at the end of Key Stages 1, 2 and 3, and so provide the basis for teachers to make their assessments. The tests are based on these descriptions.

There is a structure of years running throughout the statutory school system and four **Key Stages**. Those children who were aged five before the end of August became year 1 in the September. If they were in school before 1 September, they would have been either in a nursery class or reception. Key Stage 1 contains years 1 and 2 (infants); Key Stage 2 contains years 3 to 6 (juniors); Key Stage 3 contains years 7 to 9; and Key Stage 4 contains years 10 and 11. Sixth forms, where they exist, will contain years 12 and 13, sometimes referred to as Key Stage 5. The compulsory levels of delivery for all the NC subjects are only Key Stages 1,2 and 3. GCSEs (General Certificates of Secondary Education) and their courses are retained for Key Stage 4.

The aims of Curriculum 2000 are 'to provide opportunities for all pupils to learn and to achieve … to promote pupils' spritual, moral, social and cultural development and prepare all pupils for the opportunities, responsibilities and experiences of life' (DfEE 1999a, 1999b p. 11) and are based on a statement of values about the self, relationships, society and the environment (pp. 148, 149).

Curriculum 2000 provided an inclusive framework aiming that:

The learning across the curriculum should promote:

- spiritual, moral, social and cultural development
- personal, social and health education and citizenship
- skills development
- financial capability, enterprise education and education for sustainable development.

It also said that:

Teachers, when planning, should adapt or modify teaching and/or learning approaches and materials to provide all pupils with opportunities to succeed:

1. Setting appropriate challenges
2. Providing for the diversity of pupils' needs
3. Providing for pupils with special educational needs

4. Providing support for pupils for whom English is an additional language.

The Foundation Stage

The NC did not cover the early years (EY), reception and nursery classes. Some children are ready for the NC's programme of study for a five-year-old while they are still four, but the majority are not. Children between three and five years are said to be in the Foundation Stage. The aims of the Foundation Stage are to lay the foundations for all future learning by developing children's:

- personal, social and emotional wellbeing;
- positive attitudes and dispositions towards their learning;
- social skills;
- attention skills and persistence;
- language and communication;
- reading and writing;
- mathematics;
- knowledge and understanding of the world;
- physical development;
- creative development.

The Foundation Stage has early learning goals instead of level descriptions, to define assessment levels for the teachers.

New legislation

New legislation which came into effect in the spring of 2001 affects those schools with sixth forms, bringing the funding for these pupils under the same Learning and Skills Council regulations as pupils of 16 to 18 who go to a Sixth Form College or a Further Education College. They follow separate syllabuses for whatever qualifications they are trying to obtain.

Since the original version of the NC, IT has been renamed information and communication technology (ICT) and now includes using the Internet. ICT and RE have become part of the legally required core for all children, although English, mathematics and science are still called the core subjects. RE documents are not included within the main set of NC books, but are published separately (as a Locally Agreed Syllabus). All Community and Voluntary Controlled schools in England and Wales have to use these. Foundation and Aided Schools can make their own decisions, but have to have an agreed syllabus of some kind. Guidelines for teaching citizenship along with personal, social and health education (PSHE) became part of the NC documentation.

Subject details

You will need more details of the subjects in the Key Stages in which you are working, but you will need greater guidance than is possible here. The Further Reading section at the back of this book lists some titles which may help you in the core subject areas, although they are written for early years TAs. Your mentor will help you find what will be most useful to you. Do not try to read any of the programmes of study like a textbook.

Beginning to understand the National Curriculum

Focus

Choose a subject that interests you, or with which you are most likely to work, such as reading

Find the copy of the NC which is in your school – it will either be for primary or secondary

Reading is a subset of English

All the pages are colour coded. English is an orangey yellow colour. It starts on page 42 in the primary copy and page 44 in the secondary copy

You will find some examples of pupils' writing and some general statement about English

Turn over the pages on Speaking and Listening until you get to Reading (pages 46 and 49)

There are just three pages setting out what pupils in each relevant Key Stage should cover

Now turn to the back of book. The attainment targets are in a fold back section

Again, English has the same colour and Speaking and Listening comes first

Reading is on pages 4 and 5 respectively

These pages set out what pupils at each level should be able to do

---

In the NC document each subject is set out in the same way, and each has a different colour. Some subjects have only one part to them but English, mathematics and science all have separate parts – each with different attainment targets. Just refer to them when they are relevant or you are particularly interested. The colour codes are:

English: orangey yellow
Mathematics: deep blue
Science: scarlet red
Design and technology: green
ICT: plummy red
History: purple
Geography: brown
Art and design: orange
Music: pink
PE: Pale blue
PSHE, Citizenship, Environmental education, and Modern languages: White

The ages by which an average child is expected to reach each level is:
End of year 1: level 1
End of year 2: level 2
End of year 4: level 3
End of year 6: level 4
End of year 9: level 5
End of year 11: level 6
Brighter children reach the levels earlier, and slower learners spend longer time getting to each level.

The literacy and numeracy strategies

The twin strategies for literacy and numeracy are now part of what must be taught, and many of you may now be employed to give special support to pupils in these areas. English includes literacy – reading and writing, but it also includes speaking and listening. Some of the younger children that you may be working with find this area so difficult that they will need help with it before they will be able to read and write with any understanding. Some TAs working with the strategies will have had special training, particularly in the use of specially written materials. The literacy strategy (DfEE 1998c) was introduced into primary schools in 1998, and the numeracy strategy (DfEE 1999c) in 1999. There has been a year, 2000–2001, of piloting the introduction of the strategies to Key Stage 3, and TAs are now working with materials especially written for them for English and mathematics in year 7. Specialist guidance is needed in the use of these materials so they are not covered in this book.

The strategies have resulted in a much more formal approach to the subjects, with suggested structure to lessons, and in the case of literacy even recommended times for each part of the lesson. A more didactic, or instructional, way of class teaching has resulted, and some of you may find that your role during that class teaching time is questionable. You need to talk with your class teachers about what you should do during these class sessions. On the other hand, the group work of these structured lessons has provided a clearly defined role for TAs to work with children needing Additional Literacy Support (ALS) (DfEE 1999d). Fox and Halliwell (2000) have published a useful book to help you particularly with using the literacy and numeracy strategies. Aplin's (1998) book was recommended for TAs by the numeracy strategy.

A down side of the strategies, which have been successful in creating consistency in planning and teaching in schools, is that in some schools too much time has been spent on literacy and numeracy, squeezing out the other subjects.

Other aspects of the formal curriculum

Schools must have policies for sex education and behaviour management and can set out anything else they want to teach in their prospectuses. If you have a copy of the prospectus for the school where you work, have a look at what they say about their curriculum. They are also supposed to set out how they intend to teach this formal curriculum. Some books talk about 'delivering' the curriculum, but, clearly, delivery alone is not enough, the contents have to be understood and used. We must also recognise the importance of individual achievements, and the value both of encouraging pupils to want to learn and to value themselves and of stimulating curiosity and creativity. A challenging task!

The informal curriculum

Because the informal curriculum is not set out in legal requirements, every school will be different in this area. You will have to ask some questions (see box). The school's behaviour management policy will be important to you because it will cover how you deal with all those incidents outside the classroom.

Some questions you can ask about the informal curriculum
What clubs does the school run?
Are they in school time or after school?
Do I come to assembly? Where do I sit?
Are there places in the school where the pupils are not allowed?
Are there separate rules for the playground or the dining hall, cloakrooms or toilet areas?
What happens at wet playtimes?
What is put on walls or display shelves? Why?

As a TA you may well want to get involved in helping run one of the clubs or caring for one of the areas outside the classrooms. When you feel ready for this just ask. Many TAs have talents which may inspire a pupil to try something new, or achieve in an area not usually considered academic. This can be sporting, musical, artistic, or a hobby like stamp collecting. These areas are all of value to the pupils and the school.

The informal curriculum also includes policies covering the environment of the school, inside and out. Most schools display pupils' work and many have a formal policy saying why and how it should be displayed. It may be part of your job to help mount these displays. You will need to get to know the style used and the materials. There are techniques of mounting and various display boards which are effective in drawing attention to the work. Work is displayed for a variety of reasons. It is a sign that the school or the class teachers value the work sufficiently to show it off. The quality of the display and the time and materials used can show how significant the work is. Some schools show only the best work, and others make a policy of showing the work of all their pupils at sometime or another.

Some displays are to help the teaching of a subject. They can be posters about places or people, or diagrams of the way machines work. Pupils may help in preparing and mounting displays and this activity forms part of their curriculum. Displays can be two or three dimensional. Sometimes books or objects associated with the subject are part of the display. Always keep an eye out for displays around the school, in and out of the classrooms, at they say a lot about the school and its attitudes to learning and its pupils.

Some resource areas may become part of the informal curriculum: the library may be used for play reading, or the computer suite for a club. You may become responsible for such an area, so you will need to know how it fits in the scheme of things.

Outside, all schools have some kind of play area for breaktimes and most have some kind of grounds. Their informal curriculum will include how they want those grounds used and maintained. Environmental areas, with ponds and wild life corners, need caring for. Vandals sometimes target these areas, but where the pupils have been heavily involved in setting them up and maintaining them, they seem able to influence their outside school contacts, and the grounds stay in better condition. If you live more locally to the school than many of the teachers, you may get involved in helping look after outside study areas. Some TAs have set up such areas as projects for higher TA qualifications.

The hidden curriculum

Things that used to be implicit in the way schools worked are becoming more and more explicit, so less is 'hidden'. Things like politeness and care of property used to be taken for granted, but now sometimes have to be part of the explicit behaviour policy. Treating everybody with courtesy, whatever their needs, colour, creed or race, is spelt out in equal opportunities and anti-discrimination policies.

All schools have their own character, or climate. They try to define this in words, describing their 'ethos'. While 'to be a happy place' cannot be the first aim of a school, pupils will not learn if they are unhappy, and staff will not work with a will if they are miserable. Freiberg and Stein (1999) said:

> School climate is the heart and soul of a school. It is about that essence of a school that leads a child, a teacher, an administrator, a staff member to love the school and look forward to being there each day. School climate is about that quality of a school that helps each person feel personal worth, dignity and importance while simultaneously helping create a sense of belonging to something beyond ourselves. The climate of a school can foster resilience or become a risk factor in the lives of people who work and learn in a place called school.

It is about creating a healthy learning environment in the widest sense of the term healthy. It is about taking responsibility for one's own actions and the actions of others – for pupils as well as staff – and can lead to significant and measurable changes in attainment. Keep your eyes and ears open for ways you can contribute to this hidden curriculum.

Consider what you might mean by a healthy school

This can be done by yourself, with your teacher/mentor or with a group of colleagues.

First consider what you mean by a healthy person

You need to consider body and mind, and recognise that age or physical impairment does not prevent you being healthy

What do you need to remain healthy?

Now, think of a healthy school

You need to consider people and buildings, and recognise that age or disadvantage does not prevent the school being healthy

What does the school need to remain healthy?

Chapter 4

Assisting the learning

However clearly the curriculum is laid out in a school, teachers have to adapt their planning to meet the needs of the pupils they are going to teach, to stretch them so that they respond to the best of their ability. To do this teachers need to know how pupils learn.

Learning is complex and only partly understood even by those who spend their life trying to make sense of it. The shelves of the library are heavy with research and books explaining what is meant by learning, and how it can best happen, how to improve it or speed it up. Teaching is not just a question of 'delivering' the curriculum. The brain is not an empty jug into which knowledge can be poured.

A useful way to start trying to understand the process of learning is to look at how you yourself learn. Use the exercise to help you do this. If your colleagues are willing, ask them about their experiences.

Looking at yourself as a learner

How do you learn?

Recall a recent learning experience. It can be a formal one such as a course or evening class; a life experience such as coping with family changes, bringing up children, even divorce or bereavement; using a new piece of equipment like a new video recorder or learning to drive. The context does not matter, but you need to remember it fairly clearly.

Just jot down a few things about that experience, describing it briefly

What made you undertake it? Why did you do it? Was it necessity or whim?

Or?

What or who helped you start?

What or who helped you during the process?

What or who hindered during the process?

Was it the same all the way through? If not, how did it vary?

What else would have helped or could have been done to help you?

What feelings did you have during the process?

What skills and knowledge did you acquire?

Did anything you did or learnt relate to anything else in your life?

Have you finished? If not, will it finish?

What would you change now with hindsight?

The exercise has been used by adults on courses and some of their jottings are shown below. Were your experiences similar to these?

1. Reasons given for undertaking the learning:

new teacher — accident — thought it would be fun — thought I needed it — to keep up — needed to

2. Things people said had helped:

friends — time — previous knowledge — resources — sharing experience — fun — patience — mistakes

3. Emotions people experienced:

anxiety — frustration — challenge — fear — sense of achievement — empathy — patience — loneliness

4. Needs experienced during the learning process:

initial interest — motivation — self-determination — time and breaks, or space — commitment — structure — someone to help – a teacher (a bossy tutor was appreciated later) — a mentor — practical experience (doing) — self-discipline — social intercourse (group working, others alongside)

It is possible to draw up a set of principles with help from this exercise and lists like these. You will notice:

- Learning is not a straightforward process. It has ups and downs, and even goes backwards at times.
- People can help and hinder.
- Another person who has more experience of the same area usually is helpful – this may be a teacher or a course tutor but does not have to be.
- Other life experiences always help somewhere.
- Correct tools or words or strategies usually help.
- Time and timing is important, as are challenge and motivation.
- Most learners experience fear and anxiety as well as satisfaction.
- Attitudes to learning are important.
- Learning rarely finishes, even in a restricted area, even if the course itself does.
- We go on learning all our lives.

Trying to define learning is hard in itself. The dictionary puts the emphasis on getting more knowledge, but learning is not just about acquiring facts. One quite useful definition is:

> Learning ... that reflective activity which enables the learner to draw upon previous experience, to understand and evaluate the present, so as to shape future action and formulate new knowledge. (Abbott 1994)

One problem is that learning itself cannot be seen, only the behaviour that happens after it has taken place. There are the heart-stopping moments of seeing the 'penny drop', but these do not constitute all that is going on; most of it you cannot see.

The process of learning

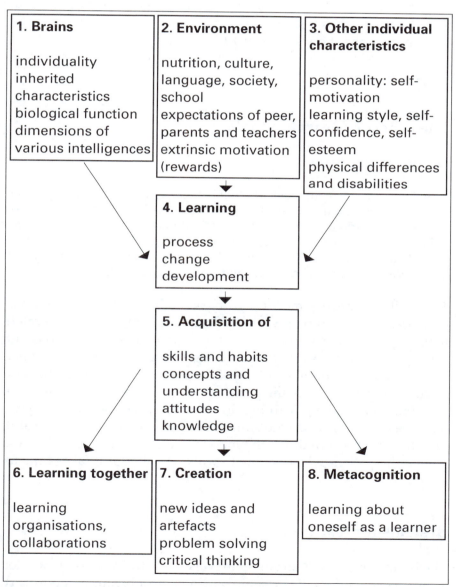

Figure 4.1   The process of learning

Figure 4.1 illustrates the process of learning and some of the factors that surround it. Thus:

1. Learning is a process of change taking place in the brain. (Human beings are animals with highly developed brains.)
2. The world around us – people and rewards – can influence how we learn.
3. The world inside us – our physical status, personality, motivation and learning style – can affect how we learn.
4. The actual process of learning – what is taking place – is a subject of much research by people trying to explain it.
5. We learn a range of things: facts (knowledge), how to do things (skills), better understanding (concepts), and about ourselves (attitudes).
6. Learning together can result in greater achievements than learning in isolation.
7. What we have learnt can lead to thinking and creating new ideas or solving problems.
8. Learning about our own way of learning can help us get better at it, and helping pupils to look at their own way of learning will help them improve too.

The inherited learning tools

The brain is made up of:

> billions of cells, (neurones). The total length of its 'wiring' between the neurones is about 100,000 kilometres (62,150 miles) ... the memory capability could be compared to 1000 CD ROMs each one containing an Encarta encyclopaedia ... the layers of organisation within the brain that act together apparently miraculously, ... handle not only memory but also vision, learning, emotion and consciousness. (Abbott 1997 p. 3)

These billions of cells meet up with each other and form enormous networks. The brain pathways between them are more complicated than any known computer and these pathways are in constant action, carrying messages (impulses) to the cells. Given the number of cells, and the number of possible pathways, the potential for learning is vast. Given the intricate layout, it is no wonder that learning and enabling learning are complex processes. If you have had a relative or friend who suffered a stroke, you will know that it may be possible to redirect the messages along different pathways, so that the patient relearns how to walk or talk. But it takes time to do so.

Systems for learning

The brain functions at all sorts of levels to control the things we do. There are the automatic systems which control breathing and heart rate – we don't have to think about these. There are the more controllable yet reflex movements such as those that enable us to escape harm. And then there are what some people call the higher order levels of brain activity, such as the emotions, our memory and thinking.

Practising is important to learning

Practising can move some activities to a more automatic or reflex level. PE routines, tables and spellings fall into this category. Some school learning needs this kind of approach: pupils repeat things in order to make them second nature. Some pupils need more repetition than others. A TA can do useful work here repeating some things with those who learn slowly, while the teacher goes on to the next thing for those who learn more quickly. Try to find different ways of tackling this to stop the repetition becoming boring. Lots of praise is needed, that is the reward. It also helps to break the tasks down into even smaller steps for some pupils; the reward is getting them to recognise that achieving each small step is a milestone for them. Schools sometimes use tangible rewards like stickers but usually real praise is enough for school work. But beware; pupils soon know if you are saying 'well done' when it isn't deserved.

When teachers draw up IEPs for children with special learning needs, this is exactly what they are doing – breaking the learning down into small steps which the learner can achieve. They set these as targets, sharing them with the pupil so that the pupil can recognise when progress has been made, and celebrate it. By working with the teacher over these IEPs, either helping to write them, sharing them with the pupils, doing the work with them or celebrating the achievement, you are helping the pupils make progress in their learning. For more detail about IEPs and the learning of youngsters with special learning needs you are recommended to read one of the specialist books in this series.

Growth and learning

The brain grows and develops like any other part of the body. There are stages in *physical* development which, as a parent, you will easily recognise or remember from your own growing up. Our *emotions* also develop, as do our ability to make relationships (*social* development), our understanding of our *culture,* and our ability to appreciate *spiritual* things.

Looking at physical child development

Get out photos or videos of your family

Can you tell by looking at these how old the children are?

Try them out on friends who do not know

What do you look for?

In the early stages, whether they can sit up or walk

You may notice how big the head is in comparison with the rest of the body

Later, whether they are wearing nappies still or how many teeth have come through

---

Thinking and learning develop as we grow, and go through stages. As with other aspects of development, the stages are not fixed. Some children never crawl; feet size can develop before height catches up. Some children talk all at once in sentences while others seem to gain a wide vocabulary first. Development can go in fits and bursts, and can sometimes seem to stay still. Piaget, an educationalist who influenced school methods for many years, studied the stages of intellectual (cognitive) development, giving them technical names which you may still hear mentioned in schools today, particularly primary or nursery schools.

Piaget's developmental stages of concept development are still useful when considering how to help children learn:

- Up to about 18 months old infants are involved in developing skills of mobility and sensing their environment; this is the 'sensori-motor stage'.
- From two to four years children are concerned only with themselves (egocentric); this is the 'pre-operational stage'.
- By about four, children are at the 'intuitive' stage – thinking logically but unaware of what they are doing.
- From seven to 11 years old, children can operate logically, but still need to see and work with real objects to learn and understand; this is the 'concrete stage'.
- Then the child is capable of 'formal' thinking about things without the 'props'; this is the 'abstract' stage.

Early learning, Piaget said, depends on using our senses: tasting, smelling, touching, seeing and hearing, and moving about to explore the world. Have you noticed how toddlers put everything in their mouths?

Early learning for the two- to four-year-old is largely practical and experience based. Children start to play together, so playgroups and nurseries help them move away from thinking only about themselves. Nursery activities are practical, acknowledging that small children need to experience the world to make sense of it, to put meaning to the words they use, before they can make sense of reading and writing and counting.

In Key Stage 1, children need practical activities, and lots of learning through play. Infant classrooms are full of apparatus and equipment. It may well be part of your job to maintain this. As you become familiar with the materials, notice when the children use the equipment. It is not just for entertaining them or keeping them quiet. Sand and water trays, role play areas, jigsaws and so on help children grasp fundamental concepts on which to build the rest of their learning.

Going from Key Stage 1 to Key Stage 2, children still need 'props' for their learning: blocks for counting, artefacts, films about days gone by. When you work with children in Key Stage 2 who have learning problems, remember their learning will depend on props much more than others in the class. They will need counters or coins to help with their calculations and pictures in their reading books to help them enjoy the stories. They still need to play with art media and have time to develop.

But it is not just slow learners who need these experiences. We need to give all children ideas and facts in stages, and provide them with props and practical experiences where possible. Even as adults we go through similar stages. We play or fiddle about with new tools or media and try things out until we have absorbed, or assimilated, the idea.

Much science work in schools is based on Piaget's ideas. There have been several research projects such as *Children Learning in Science* (Driver 1983), *Really Raising Standards* (Adey and Shayer (1994) and SPACE research (Russell *et al.* 1991) to look at the way young people learn science. The science teachers in your school may be able to discuss these ideas with you. The well used series Science 5-13 (Schools Council (1980)) and the Nuffield Primary Science series (1993) may well still be on staffroom shelves, both were based on these ideas of concept and development.

Learning styles

There are differences in the physical make-up of individual brains, even in identical twins. It is also believed that different parts of the brain engage in different ways of thinking or learning. Gardner *et al.* (1996) suggests that there is not just one intelligence, but seven. Thus there are different intelligences for different things but you can be good in more than one area. Try out the list of Gardner's intelligences on yourself.

Gardner's intelligences

Verbal/linguistic: Do you think in words? Do you have to talk or write things down to sort them out?

Logical/mathematical: Do you like things organised? Are you good at numbers?

Visual/spatial: Do you think in pictures? Do you like diagrams? Can you visualise things easily when you read about them?

Bodily/kinaesthetic: Are you good at PE? Have people described you as agile or the opposite – clumsy?

Musical/rhythmic: Are you musical? Do you like dancing? Do you work better with music playing in the background?

Interpersonal: Do you get on well with other people? Do you form relationships easily? Do you work better with others?

Intrapersonal: Can you work things out for yourself or do you have to always involve others? Are you comfortable with yourself? Can you work on your own?

If you can find out how you work best you can use that method when you have to learn something new. You can also try to develop aspects of yourself that you feel are weak. So if you are not good at working with others you might try to develop this skill. If you are musical, you may find it easier to learn with music playing, or you might even turn a list of things you have to learn into a song!

Likewise, it might be helpful for the pupils you work to sort out their strengths and weaknesses. Talk to them about it. Lazear (1994) has some useful checking lists designed for children of different ages to complete themselves, using smiley faces for the younger ones. His book is full of little exercises and explanations of these various intelligences. The idea is that if we know what mode the pupils are operating in we can support them better.

The influence of environment

Outside influences can also affect how our learning develops. For example, differences in language affect how we communicate, and the words we use. Even English language vocabulary differs between the United Kingdom and the United States. Children from homes where there are few books and little discussion are likely to have a restricted vocabulary. They may not be able to label and describe as many things and ideas as children from families where self-expression is encouraged. Similarly they may be less fluent with grammar and structure. One of the important roles a TA can play is to extend children's vocabulary and enable them to express their views and ideas better.

Changes of background, language or culture can create barriers to learning. Names you may hear in the staffroom will include Bernstein, Bruner and Vygotsky (Wood 1988). Changes in routines can affect day-to-day learning. Even things like the goldfish dying or Auntie coming to stay can upset the learning process for some pupils. This means you need to be sensitive to the background of the pupils you work with. You cannot change their circumstances, but if you are aware of them you will have a greater understanding of the pupil's learning needs. It may be that you are the one member of staff they can confide in when they cannot concentrate, or seem tired or off colour. Do remember to tell the teacher you are working with if you are at all bothered by what a pupil tells you, or if you think the problem is likely to be a long-standing one.

Social interaction or lack of it can affect learning. As we have seen, this may be a language problem; but it is also about relating to other people, learning with and from them, and communicating. Playgroups and nurseries help children develop socially before they come into mainstream school, where for so much of their time they are confined to a desk or table. As a TA, working with small groups you are an important factor in helping pupils develop both social skills to enable them to get on with one another and social awareness to help them learn.

Other influences on learning

Special needs
If we are tired or ill it can be hard to learn, even just to read. Children and young people with a physical disability are liable to have to spend effort and time in dealing with the disability – effort and time that the able bodied can put into learning. All who work with pupils with special educational needs of a physical origin will be familiar with the effects these disabilities can have. Your role will be to

provide the support that takes away some of the hassle their physical condition brings, so that they can use their mental powers to the full. In the photograph a TA is transporting an able pupil over lengthy distances between teaching areas. Once in the teaching area he can concentrate on what he has to do and cope with the walking necessary in the classroom.

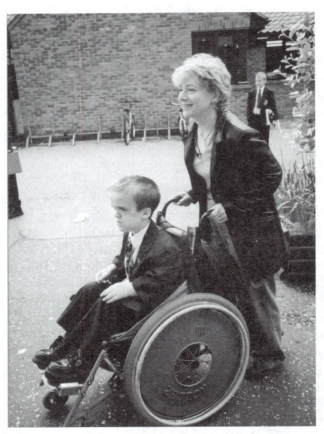

Helping a student to keep all his energies for the classroom

There are also children whose brains are damaged or under-developed. This may prevent them from thinking and learning properly. Try to discuss these two types of physical disability with the class teacher whose class has SEN children in it, or the SENCO. Children with a physical impairment can think and learn as well as other children if they are given the appropriate support. But a different kind of help is needed for children with brain damage. Fortunately, much can now be done to assist their learning.

Emotional development
Emotional development and conditions affect learning. Feelings can get in the way, and pupils – even bright ones – who are bored, insecure or preoccupied by other problems, will not perform well. Younger children are less able to control these emotions, and teenagers' control systems are affected by hormones. You can be of

great help to the learning situation by providing an understanding ear to pupils in distress. Be careful when dealing with confidences; this is dealt with in greater depth in Chapter 6.

Motivation

Motivation is one of the greatest influences on learning. The will to achieve can overcome many physical and social handicaps. Look at the effort which goes into the paraplegic Olympics. Setting up a home of one's own can make 'DIY' experts of even the most impractical people. The opposite also applies: when one becomes bored it is difficult to concentrate or persevere. Even easy tasks become a chore.

One of the skills you can develop is to find out the interests of your pupils, and build upon them. Find a football annual, a handbook on guinea pig care or get an Internet guide, if that is what they want to read about. Always keep a note of any changes you make and share them with the teacher.

Self-confidence and self-esteem

This was sometimes overlooked in the past. We all have stories from our own schooldays of the teacher who was demeaning of our efforts. A put-down can occasionally motivate a pupil to achieve despite the comment, but the memory of discomfort stays. Many others are prevented by failure, or even perceived failure, from trying a second time. Show how to do things by example, but don't try to overwhelm pupils with your own talent! Fox (2001 pp. 19–31) and Hook and Vass (2000 pp. 22–38) both include whole chapters on the importance of self-esteem and strategies to support it. Some suggestions for raising and maintaining the self-esteem of your pupils are given in the box.

Here's one I did earlier …

Do you use any of these strategies which could raise self-esteem?

Talk to everyone the same way, regardless of gender, race or background

Address pupils by their preferred name

Use positive comments – 'thank you for walking' – 'well done for being quiet', including written comments if you can – 'well read today' – 'I liked the story'

Use praise appropriately, not indiscriminately

Treat boys and girls equally, whether for tasks or treats or even lining up

Provide a good role model in gender, culture and disability, both in reality and when finding examples in teaching materials such as books and magazines

Use rewards, praise and congratulation systems for work, including showing it to other staff

Catch them being good or working hard and tell them

Set small achievable targets and congratulate them on achieving them

Have reward systems for behaviour – telling the teachers about the good as well as the troublesome

Value work by ensuring it is taken care of, and presented well, both by you and the pupil

Encourage independence appropriate to age and maturity

Enable and encourage peer tutoring

Use humour carefully

Encourage children to value their own performance

Listen to the views of pupils and act on them where possible

Avoid being patronising or sarcastic as pupils recognise both.

Can you add to this?

Independent learning

It is important that pupils you are helping do not become dependent on you. If you do the task for them, all they learn is that someone will do it if they wait around long enough. Your role is to enable them to do it for themselves. You must look towards their potential not just what they can or cannot do at that point in time.

If you can see the potential learning of a child you can put in place steps to bring them up to the next stage. This is sometimes referred to as 'scaffolding'. You can help this process by searching out the patterns and being ready with the right steps at the right time. You may be able to supply a missing bit in their understanding, or find a different word for something the teacher has said, which enables the pupil to understand the content of the lesson or perform the task better. The important thing for the pupil is that you provide the scaffolding not build the complete tower for them. Seeing what is needed to move a pupil's learning on to the next level comes with experience – from knowing the curriculum objective and the way the pupil learns, and putting the two together. Some TAs have even described 'doing myself out of a job' as part of their role.

Observing learning

One of the exciting things when working with children is to see that 'penny drop' moment, but it is only part of the story. Learning is built up from lots of little pieces. Educational psychologists spend much time trying to work out the learning patterns of children who are struggling with school work. This can be a fascinating area, but recognise there are no easy answers or short cuts. Just keep watching, listening and learning more about learning.

Try spending a little time watching other learners. To do this you will need the co-operation of a class teacher with whom you can discuss the issues and protocols of observation. You will notice all sorts of things at random, just by being in a busy classroom, but it will sharpen your perceptions if you do this with some organisation. It means either taking time out of your paid time or using your own time. It is important that your observing does not become intrusive for the pupil. You will need to make some notes, and this means making records on someone else's child, and for whom a class teacher is responsible. These matters must not be taken lightly, so you need some agreed ground rules covering, for example:

- the purpose of your observation;
- confidentiality of things said;
- ownership of things written;
- what is left unsaid – honesty and integrity will help;
- ethical factors involved by mentioning others in your school or family;
- whether names are to be used or records to be anonymised;
- what happens to any discussions or records;

A possible checklist is shown in the box.

Possible protocols to consider for classroom observation

The following needs to be discussed between the TA and the class teacher where any observation is to take place:

- The purpose of the exercise is to... (e.g. understand more about)
- The adults involved will be...
- The pupils involved will be...

The head teacher/department head/line manager has been told what is happening, and has agreed.

It needs to be checked that:

- Anything written is shared first with the teacher for comments to be made and points of accuracy checked.

- Any comments to be seen by others will be anonymised, or amalgamated with others to preserve confidentiality.
- The main audience of any summary written material would be... (e.g. the other member of a course, or an outside reader).
- The people observed or interviewed can have a copy of the notes made if they so wished.
- You know what will happen to any written records.
- The intended outcome of the activity is...
- You know what you will do if the observation shows up anything within the classroom or school that someone wishes to address or celebrate.
- If others get involved, they would be covered by the same sort of protocols.
- Someone seeks permission of the parents of the children closely involved.

Either side should be able to make comment at any time in the process if there is any discomfort or suggestion about what is taking place or being said.

There are books which cover why, what, where and how to observe, such as Wragg (1994) – although this was written for teachers – and Harding and Meldon Smith (1996). This latter book was written for NVQ (National Vocational Qualification) students in Child Care and so is a more helpful book for TAs. Even though written primarily for those working with the EY, its principles hold good throughout school phases, and the suggested forms are very useful. These books also look at things you can measure about learning and things that you cannot, but which are equally important. Practically, you will need a means of writing and something to record on. A sheet of A4 paper on a clipboard will do, or a spiral bound memo pad. Probably the most difficult decision is where to start, with so many things happening at once in any classroom. The trick is to focus on one area of interest and observe at regular times. The exercises in the boxes should get you started.

Observing a pupil (1)

Remembering the protocols of observing, with the agreement of the class teacher and, if possible, the pupil you watch:

- Decide on a pupil to watch
- Decide on a part of their body which is of interest – their hands? What they are saying?
- Note what is happening every minute on the minute for five minutes
- Did they keep still? Did they touch any resources? Did they touch another pupil?

- Who did they speak to? Was it about their work?
- Did this tell you anything more about the pupil, the table or desk they are working on, the children they are with?

Repeat the exercise with a different pupil at the same desk/table, or the same pupil in a different context or classroom.

Observing a pupil (2)

Remembering the protocols of observing, with the agreement of the teacher and, if possible, the pupil:

- Mark out a sheet of A4 with headings for five-minute intervals covering half an hour
- Choose a pupil that you are not working directly with
- Note every five minutes what they are doing, and, if they are talking and you can hear what they say, put that down

What have you found out about this pupil?

Observation is often the way to 'catch a pupil being good'. If you are observing a pupil who is frequently a problem, notice what they were occupied with when they were not distracting someone else. When they are distracting others, note down what started it off, and what makes it worse or better. You can develop grids with names and headings of what you are particularly looking for, like asking or answering questions, or with time markers. There is a simple grid in the *Teaching Assistant File* (DfEE 2000a and DfES 2001a).

After you have done the observation, ask yourself the questions in the box.

After observing

What did the pupil do during that period?

Was it anything to do with what the teacher intended or not?

Did the pupil learn anything new during the time you were watching?

Did they understand anything better?

Did they practise anything that they had done before?

Did anyone talk to them or help them?

If so, were these people sitting near them or adults?

Could you have made things easier for them if you had been sitting there, or if they had been in a different place, or had different resources?

In what ways?

Find an opportunity to talk through what you saw with the teacher.

What is learnt?

It might seem easier to observe and measure what is learnt over a period of time rather than try to watch it actually happening but it has its pitfalls. Test results depend very much on how questions are asked, particularly where understanding is needed as well as memory recall, such as in a subject like science. Pictures, and seeing or being able to handle the materials about which questions are asked – even being able to ask questions about the meaning of the questions – all alter how correct the answers may be.

Teachers plan for a particular outcome and therefore know what they are looking for. Work with the teacher to understand this and you too will be able to see when those you are helping have 'got there'. By practising and refining your observations of learning, in a particular area or with a particular child, you can record what you have seen, and give valuable feedback to the teacher. This means teachers *can* have eyes in the backs of their heads, can teach and keep a check on the pupils, can do two things at once.

The outcomes of learning are not all factual knowledge. Most important is the understanding that goes with the facts. There are the skills and habits that come from repeating tasks, from practising. A musician or gymnast, a carpenter or mechanic will tell you of the hours they have spent perfecting skills, however talented they are in the field. It is also important to look at pupils' attitudes to learning.

Learning together

Interestingly, when two or three people are working together, the result can be better than their individual efforts might produce. People working in groups or teams can bounce ideas off one another; come with different learning styles, different sets of competencies and skills, experiences and knowledge bases which contribute to the whole. Individual learning is essential, but joint learning can be not only productive but exciting, developmental and creative. This is true for the children and adults.

It is important to distinguish whether children in a group are all doing a similar but individual task or whether they are doing a collaborative task where each member can contribute something to the whole. In the first of these, more work may be done if there is silence, but in the second, talking together is essential. Working with groups is dealt with in Chapter 5.

Creating new ideas

The areas of thinking, creativity and problem solving are ones where there is a lot of debate. Some teachers feel the legally required National Curriculum or the schools' syllabuses leave little time for these activities. Many teachers ensure they earmark time or provide after school activities which give opportunities for these areas to be covered. While not all learning needs to result in creative or problem-solving activity, it is here that the greatest achievements of human beings are born. Without these activities, there would have been no civilisations, no progress, no arts or technical advances. It is important to establish with the class teacher to what extent you may allow the pupils you are working with to deviate from the task in hand if they get a good idea.

Learning about learning

If we can recognise how we best learn – our style – we can build on that knowledge. We can also train ourselves to improve. It is partly about understanding the different intelligences mentioned before, but it is also about all the other pieces in the learning jigsaw: when help is needed, whether there are emotional or physical things stopping the process, what kind of tools, books or equipment will help with a task, what kind of words might help.

Learning about learning is called **metacognition.** You can help your pupils to recognise how they best learn. You can recognise your own learning patterns and watch for patterns in the pupils with whom you work. Try talking to the children about what you have seen. Use phrases like 'Do you know you are not reading through your written work?', 'Where do you do your homework?', 'Would singing your spellings help you learn them?'.

Difficult things to measure are how pupils learn and their attitudes to learning. Inspectors attempt to do this, under the heading of how well the pupils are taught. They look at the extent to which pupils:

Using your understanding to assist learning

- acquire new knowledge or skills, develop ideas and increase their understanding;

- apply intellectual, physical or creative effort in their work;

- are productive and work at a good pace;

- show interest in their work, are able to sustain concentration and think and learn for themselves;

- understand what they are doing, how well they have done and how they can improve. (Ofsted 1999 p. 46)

To help assist learning you can:

- try to understand more about your own learning styles;
- provide opportunities for repetition and reinforcement, vocabulary and scaffolding;
- learn more about the social, cultural or emotional context in which the pupils are operating;
- find out more about the individual needs of the pupils with whom you are working closely;
- find out what experiences the learners have already had or what they might have missed;
- learn something of the subjects which they are learning for yourself, so that you know what might be coming next, or know what an appropriate strategy for that subject might be;
- notice what kind of learning styles pupils have and talk with them about their own learning;
- value pupils and their learning, appreciate what individuals have achieved and tell them – to boost their self-esteem;
- be authentic, open, with pupils and adults;
- ensure you know what is the learning intention of the teacher;
- assist in creating a positive learning environment, both in the material surroundings and in attitudes to work and one another;
- become part of the learning organisation that is your school, share your ideas and listen to others;
- apply your learning to the situation in which you find yourself;
- have high expectations of the pupils, yourself and learning standards.

Chapter 5

Supporting teaching

We all teach at some time. Parents teach their children, children teach other children. But by 'teachers', the government, the general public, and more particularly the media are referring to adults with qualified teacher status. Most dictionary definitions of teaching can be applied to the work of TAs, but they could also be used about many other categories of people interacting with children. We need to look at educational definitions. Ask your TA and teacher colleagues what they mean by 'teaching'. They may use the word 'pedagogy', the art or study of teaching. Watkins and Mortimore (1999) define pedagogy as 'any conscious activity by one person designed to enhance the learning in another' (p. 3). But this again is a general definition which could fit many people, and is not necessarily associated with schools.

Teachers may refer you to the definition used by Ofsted inspectors. While these inspectors are not required to look directly at the work of TAs in the classroom using their framework, some do so, and have remarked that TAs can score highly using similar criteria to those used for teachers. Another definition worth looking at can be found in the published standards for qualified teachers. These make it clear there is much more to being a teacher than the front-of-class role; but they are detailed and, for some, controversial.

Books by Kyriacou (1986; 1991) and Dunne and Wragg (1994) are helpful in working out with teachers the nature of your job with them. You may find these in your staffroom, or teacher colleagues may have a copy to lend. It isn't necessary to read them in detail, but both contain some useful definitions and tasks to do, as well as amusing drawings and helpful photographs. If your teachers are familiar with them, ask them which bits they found helpful.

Remember that the classroom teacher must lead in setting out the objectives of the lessons and the strategies by which these can be achieved, provide the role model, and direct the activities. Given this lead, you can assist in all of these areas, provided you and the teacher are agreed about your boundaries. TAs do teach, but do not carry the responsibility for the direction and organisation of the learning.

What is teaching?

The teaching processes

Hopkins (1995) described teaching as an integration of models, skills and artistry (see Figure 5.1).

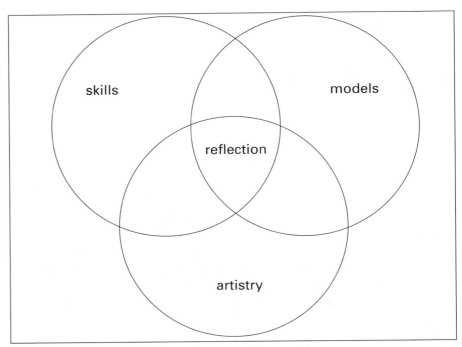

Figure 5.1　The processes involved in teaching

Models

The term 'models' refers to different teaching approaches, such as:

- didactic or instructional – the 'stand up in front of a group and tell them' approach;
- group working – pupils of the same ages (peers) co-operating to further their learning;
- creative – allowing pupils to create, experiment and investigate beyond the set work;
- mechanical – encouraging the memorising of things like spellings or tables, or old-fashioned 'object' lessons;

and so on. It is generally agreed that all teachers need to use a combination of styles or approaches to tackle the variety of subjects they teach and pupils' various needs. This is how they achieve the 'match' between the pupils and the curriculum. The literacy and numeracy strategies (see Chapter 3) include all these various approaches through the 'hour' or 'lesson'.

You are unlikely to need to use these different styles, since you will not be dealing with whole classes or whole lessons. But try to watch various teachers at work and see how they approach their teaching. Is it different for different subjects? For instance, do drama or PE teachers favour one approach, or science or technology teachers another? Do the teachers of younger children teach in the same way as the teachers of older children?

Artistry

Artistry is about using personality and relationships to create the right learning atmosphere for the situation. For some, it appears completely instinctive – maybe these are the 'born teachers'. On the other hand, artistry can be cultivated and developed by those teachers and TAs who are themselves learners – those who reflect upon their own practice and continually refine what they do.

Your personality

Never underestimate the effect you as a TA have on a classroom climate just by being you. Watching TAs at work with children and young people, it is clear that the way they relate to the pupils has a powerful effect on the learning. You need to be *sensitive* to changes in pupils' moods, and to respond appropriately.

A TA is a role model for learning and can show that learning never stops. You also offer a role model for good manners, for care of equipment, for the way you organise the resources, for the way you talk to one another. Even your speech and handwriting offer exemplars, hopefully of the way the school wants their pupils to go.

The following are characteristics of TAs that have been noted in the classroom. Do they describe you?

1. *Enthusiasm*

   Your enthusiasm, interest and love of your job, your enjoyment of their company alone can improve the interest and enjoyment for pupils and their motivation.

2. *Listening skills*

   Can you listen? For some children just having someone to talk to can make all the difference.

3. *Self-confidence*

   Your confidence – acting it, even if you are scared underneath – helps promote the pupils' own self-esteem and self-confidence. If you are relaxed and smile, it will look as though you know what you are doing and like it (even if you do not).

4. *Commitment*

   Are you totally committed to the task in hand? Lesson time is not to be used for thinking of the next meal, or when the library books are due back, or the results of tonight's match. The pupils and the lesson objectives are what matters for the duration of the time you are with the pupils. Your concentration and perseverance will encourage pupils to persist.

5. *Empathy and sympathy*

   Your empathy, and, when needed, sympathy can ease pupils' tensions, your respect can give them a sense of being important. Your experience of small children or empathy for teenagers can be a helpful addition to the class climate, particularly if you are a parent and the class teacher is not.

6. *Initiative*

Using your own initiative is a careful balancing act. There must be appropriate boundaries with your classroom teacher, yet it is helpful if you are able to get on with things without constantly consulting them. Be open with the teachers, and ask if it is all right to use your judgement. Remember, different teachers may want to establish different boundaries. Some may want their pupils to ask them before leaving the room for the toilet, and others are quite happy for you to deal with giving this permission. Some will want you to help yourself to resources, others will want to allocate them to you. Check what is expected of you in terms of behaviour management and adapting tasks. Your relationship with the teacher will become easier with time, as you become used to each other's ways.

7. *Sense of humour*

One advantage of your limited responsibilities is that you may be more relaxed than the teachers; your sense of humour eases some of those otherwise tight situations that can occur in all classrooms and schools. A TA can support a teacher who is suffering stress, personal or school induced, like before an inspection.

Relationships

Relationships are crucial. Your friendliness to pupils *must* be offered in a professional context, but it could be a lifesaver. You have to maintain a professional distance, not letting yourself become emotionally involved with a child's circumstances while understanding the issues. This may need practice and reflection. One of the problems of being allocated to an individual pupil can be forming too close a relationship. Remember, one of your tasks is to enable pupils to stand on their own feet, to go home at the end of the day, week or term without you, and cope. You need to cultivate a climate of mutual respect.

Physical contact

The pitfalls of having too close a contact are dealt with in Chapter 6, under the child protection section. But often a TA can provide comfort to children in stressful personal situations. Parents could be separating, a house move may be imminent, the child may have fallen out of favour with a friend, or have a newborn brother or sister. For the older pupils trying to cope with the hormone changes of puberty, the TA can become another adult to argue with. Often, simply sitting closely alongside a child gives reassurance and helps their concentration sufficiently to enable them to get on with a task or listen to the teacher talking. For learners lacking confidence, particularly the younger ones, the close presence is reassuring. You must be sensitive, particularly if you are linked with an individual child for several years, and change as they change.

Remember that any close contact of this kind can also label a child as needing help. This can be a real drawback to their developing independence. In secondary schools, this presence can become irksome and self-defeating. It will need your close co-operation with the teachers to ensure your presence is helpful and not hindering. You may want to suggest working with a group rather than an individual, working with other children but within call, or placing yourself where you can observe and then move in to help only when the pupil's attention wanders. If you are employed as a 'minder' for a behaviourally challenging pupil, you will need to work out your strategies carefully after full discussion with the SENCO, and where possible with individual class teachers too. One helpful strategy, in primary or secondary classrooms, is to negotiate time in class when you are not directly responsible for the named pupil, but are doing something else and observing the pupil. At some point, you will 'catch them being good'. Make a note of the circumstances, when and why it happened and reflect on your findings with the teacher and SENCO, and, if possible, the pupil concerned.

Behaviour management

Behaviour management is not something that happens on its own. You do not 'get the children well-behaved, then teach'! Managing behaviour is about creating a climate in which teaching takes place; it affects everything you do. It is about adopting attitudes and strategies which are consistent throughout both classroom and school for all children, not just those who have particular problems. You can develop techniques and language, and practise skills, which support whatever the policy is in your school. Use them throughout the lesson, and throughout any informal times in other areas of the school as well. If you are working with disturbed children, or children who are on identified SEN stages for problems with behaviour, you must certainly consult the SENCO or class teacher for help in this area. Most authorities are now running courses to help TAs with specialised techniques.

Skills and classroom activity

Whatever you are involved in as a TA, in or away from the classroom, you are under the guidance of the class teacher. If in doubt as to whether any course of action or strategy is appropriate, always ask.

Facilitating learning

The vital technique when working with learners of any age is to understand something of them as learners. That is why learning had a chapter of its own. Whatever the teacher asks you to do with the pupils, after finding out the objectives you can make a difference.

The interface between learning and teaching is cloudy. A good teacher is always aware of the learning needs of the class, and adapts the teaching programme to match those needs. Those needs may relate to ways in which the pupils learn, or to physical, emotional, social, cultural or spiritual differences.

Some of the ways in which we adapt what we do are instinctive, because of our personality. Some of us are better at empathising with people than others are. This could be because we have brought up a family, or have worked with learners before, and have noticed what helps or doesn't. The tendency when starting as a TA is to operate merely as a 'keeper' or 'task minder', ensuring the pupils keep their 'nose to the grindstone'. Your role can be so much more than that.

MacGilchrist *et al.* (1997) have a helpful diagram (Figure 5.2) in their book *The Intelligent School* where they talk about the teacher and learner making a learning pact. If you add a TA to the classroom the dynamics change (Figure 5.3). Another way of looking at this is shown in Figure 5.4.

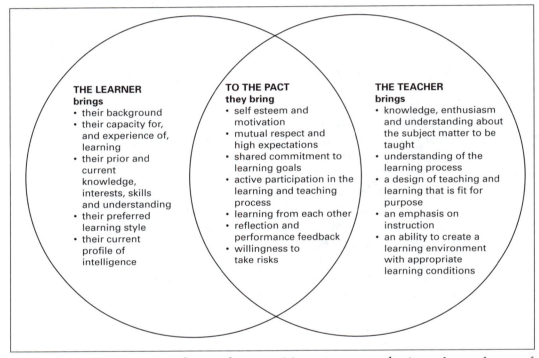

Figure 5.2   The teaching and learning pact: the interdependence of the teacher and learner

It is worth spending time with the teachers you work most closely with, exploring what their expectations of your work are, and how they will enable you to perform to your best. In this way, everyone is clear about your role. When things are not talked about misunderstandings can arise. You could use Figure 5.4 and talk it through with your mentor or teacher, and establish with them where the boundaries lie for you. There is also a useful simple questionnaire in Fox (1998 p. 39) which you can each use on your own and then compare notes. This gives suggestions of how things might be able to change for the better.

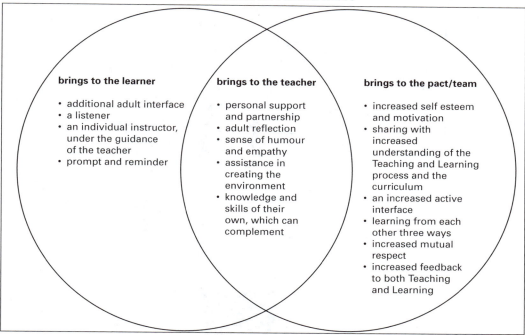

Figure 5.3 The teaching and learning pact with the teaching assistant

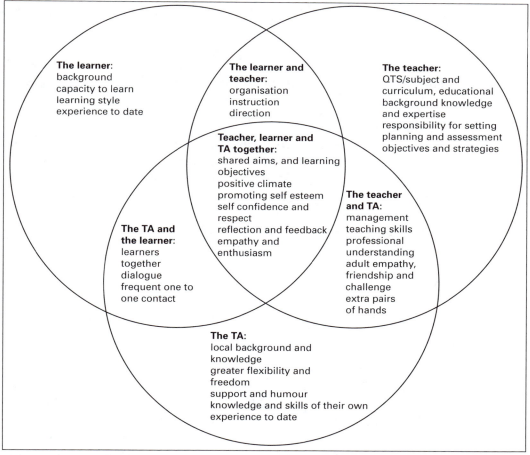

Figure 5.4 The interactions of teachers, TAs and pupils in the classroom

The performance despite the distracting thoughts

Performance

Teaching is a performance, an act. All professions have an acting role to a degree. Think of the barrister in court, or the consultant doing a ward round. Being 'professional' means that when you arrive at your place of work, you put the cares of your domestic and personal life as far out of your mind as you can, and concentrate on the job for which you are being paid. It can be a hard act, if things at home have gone wrong, or there is a personal crisis. Some serious crises such as illness of your child, or a close bereavement, may hinder your effectiveness, and some even demand your absence from school to deal with them.

Teaching demands courage, forethought and practice. Be clear about the role you have to play.

1. Dressing the part

    You will have found out if there a dress code in your school. Look at the other staff, if there is no written code. This does not mean submerging your personality; it is preparing your part. Thus high heels may make you feel smart but may not be helpful to the active role you will be playing. An overall or apron might be useful for some lessons, and you will be setting an example to the pupils you work with if you are prepared for this.

2. Culturing a 'presence'

   The way you walk and talk should show the pupils that you carry some authority: they should identify you as a member of staff. One of the problems TAs may have is being labelled by the pupils as a 'non-teacher'. TAs have fought for recognition, to prove they are not a 'non'-anything. Pupils pick up unspoken messages of 'presence' very easily. Your words, gestures and stance when asking pupils to do something should convey that you mean what you say and have sufficient authority to say it. This does not mean you should be aggressive. If you appear confident and relaxed, sure that you have a right and proper place in the scheme of things in the school, you will earn respect. Try never to appear nervous or anxious, however shaky you may be inside.

3. Communicating clearly

   Speech needs to be clear, grammatically correct, and delivered with a firm but not loud tone of voice. This may need practice on your part. It should not be about accent. However, this can be a sensitive area for some school staff and it is difficult for managers to deal with if there are problems: speech seems so personal a trait to be commenting on. But staff in school have to set an example, in speech as well as dress. Where the English language is the subject to be taught, correct oral examples do help. You could try tape recording yourself, and listening to it played back. That is how you sound to others. If necessary, you can practise a few simple changes.

4. Manner and body language

   Your manner and the way you use gestures are also important. A lot of subtle behaviour management can be achieved without words. Signalling 'turn it down' can be effective while eye contact can sometimes tell a miscreant he or she is observed, or bring a dreamer back to task. Never appear bored, even if you are, as it only creates an atmosphere of boredom for others. Good manners and respect for other staff and pupils will engender their respect, and encourage their good manners towards you and one another.

5. Know your audience

   Learn the names of the pupils you work with as soon as you can. It helps communication and control, and gives the children a sense of their individuality.

6. Organise

   Keep a constant eye on the time it you are in charge of an activity. Give a shape to the activity within the overall time allowed: beginning, middle and end. Recognise the various 'scenes in the act'. Pace is crucial, and ensuring the flow of any task keeps up the pupil's interest.

Performance is hard work, and needs consistency, but is worth the effort. Once you are established in your role you will then find that should something go wrong – say you lose your voice – the pupils are sympathetic and co-operative, and do not take advantage of you.

Exposition: instructing, explaining, describing

Having got your role sorted, you need to prepare your material. This may be a list of things you want to say, but it will also include any examples you are going to use.

What is your aim? It may be to convey a set of facts, to give reasons or ideas. You may want to promote thinking in the area the teacher is covering. This may show itself in pupils' questions.

Structure and prepare your material (see box), even practise in front of a mirror. Most teachers and lecturers have tried this at one time or another. You may only be doing a five-minute slot to four children on using clay for the first time, but there are still things you need to tell them regarding safety, cleanliness or what they are going to make.

Exposition

Try to put your ideas in a logical sequence, and if possible note the key points. Try to have a beginning, middle and end

Find the right words, speak clearly, watch the tone and inflections in your voice

Be sure of what you need to say or do – not too many 'ums' and 'ers'

Try to involve the pupils. Television presenters try to do this, even without a live audience. Just watch a *Blue Peter* presenter: their eyes, their pace, their pauses. It all looks 'off the cuff', but is the result of practice

Get the pupils' attention, maintain eye contact when you can. Use appropriate gestures

Explain what you are going to do or cover, and what the pupils should get out of it – or learn

Try to get their interest from the start. Find out what they already know in the area if you have time, as this provides the scaffolding for the learning you are trying to promote.

Where you can, link what you are saying to other lessons they have had in the same area, or what the teacher is particularly wanting to do. Even if you are working separately with pupils with SEN, try to make what you are doing relate to what the rest of the class are doing to allow them to keep up.

Emphasise the important bits. You may have to adapt as you go along, so be sensitive to the way in which the pupils are reacting to you and what you are saying. This will help you decide the next step, or how large a jump you can make in assuming understanding

Use examples or analogies, objects or pictures, maps,

---

diagrams, sounds, anything to create curiosity, motivate or add interest. Have a 'here is one I made earlier' item ready if that is relevant

Draw or put key words down as you go along; you may even get to use the blackboard, whiteboard or overhead projector. Make sure you have paper, pencils, pens or chalk if you are going to need them. Do not get up to get things; this is an ideal opportunity for any pupils to lose interest or to become disruptive

Try to get feedback, and promote discussion again if you have time. Did they understand what you were talking about? Dialogue keeps them both awake and participating. Respond to them

Try to leave time to get one pupil to recall what you have been saying to another pupil. This helps them clarify their mind and also gives you an idea how well they have taken things in

Summarise at the end.

Find a teacher you admire and watch how they explain a point. A mentor relationship with this skill is particularly helpful, where someone you respect will watch you and comment on how you do it. You may even get brave enough to be videoed so that you can watch yourself.

Questioning and challenging

This is one of the most important ways in which you can help children learn, achieve, think, and question for themselves. Teachers use questions:

1. To encourage thought and ideas: As children get older, this will also encourage them to challenge systems and values. For some, this may sound like opening up a 'can of worms' – 'surely school is about imparting knowledge not challenging ideas'. Education is about both for, without knowledge and understanding, any questioning is superficial; without questioning, how can we be sure we understand or make any progress?

2. Purely to check knowledge and understanding: Questions may be oral and everyday ('what do you want for breakfast?'), or factual ('what do you know about Columbus?'), difficult ('how are shadows made?'), or instructional ('do you remember what I told you about the playground?').

3. As a teaching strategy: Selecting questions that one or two students may be able to answer may be used to break up the teacher's monologue and increase the participation of the group. Watch and listen to your class teacher. They will ask questions at various levels of difficulty to encourage all the children to feel able to answer and thus participate.

Questioning

Questions

Collect questions over a lesson – with the permission of the teacher – and see if you can classify them. You can do this in several ways.

- Why were the questions asked? To probe understanding, to query knowledge recall, to prompt pupils otherwise losing concentration?
- What sort of answers did the questions elicit? Yes/no? A fact or two? Puzzled faces? A variety of answers, all of which could be right?
- Which pupils could have answered each question? How hard were they?
- Which pupils did answer?
- What range of ideas was covered in the one lesson?

Questions which need only a yes/no answer or have only one correct answer are called **closed** questions, and those that could have various correct answers are **open** questions. Open questions require more thought on the part of the respondent, and are sometimes called 'higher order' questions. They need more reasoning, maybe analysis or evaluation of a situation, and usually more time for the respondent to give the answer. In a large class situation there is not time for open questions – but you as a TA with a small group may have the time and opportunity to use them. Questioning, like the other skills, needs practice. If you know beforehand the task you are to perform, you can prepare some searching questions in advance.

Asking questions needs just the same kind of clarity, eye contact, and structure as an exposition, but the timing is more crucial. When do you put in the question? How long do you wait for an answer? What do you do if no-one answers or if they all call out at once? You may need a strategy like 'hands up' even with a small group, or you can ask a pupil by name.

Do you correct a child who gives a wrong answer to a closed question, or do you ask others and seek a consensus? What sort of praise will you give for a right answer? What if a child answers with another question? (Listen to politicians, they are adept at this!) Can you challenge the answer to an open-ended question? If you asked 'What do you hope to do at the weekend?', you can follow it up with phrases like 'Well, what will happen if it rains?'

Children often ask quite difficult question: 'How do seagulls glide?', 'Why is there oil underground?', 'Why is water wet?', 'Why does glue stick?'. Never be afraid to say 'I don't know' or 'I am not sure, how do you think we can find out?'. Finding out the answers together, or sending the pupil off to look something up, or asking an expert, are actions which set children off on the quest for knowledge. Some questions have no absolutely correct answer but form part of life's imponderables. They will ask at some time 'Who is God?', 'What happens when you die?'. Think about how you answer these in our multicultural society.

Assessing and recording in class

All the time you work with pupils you are inwardly making small judgements. Can they do what you ask easily or quickly? Have they understood? Are they enjoying what you are doing? Should you do it differently next time? Keep these thoughts going, this is the essence of good teaching and will form the basis of the way you adjust what you do to the needs of your group. Occasionally, the teacher may ask your opinion of what went on, or ask you to make notes as you go along.

If you do make notes, remember these are comments about the pupils. Ensure they are accurate. If possible, pupils should know what you are writing about them, and what you are going to do with the notes. All notes should be treated as confidential and either given to the teacher or kept appropriately. If notes are to be used for a study or course, you should have the permission of the pupil to use them – or their parents if the pupils are young – and all names should be changed in any written work you hand in to a college or tutor. This is called anonymising the data.

Using resources or equipment

Make sure you have these ready before you work with the pupils, unless getting out the equipment is part of their task. This may be so in science or PE. Resources should be of the highest quality that is available. You and the equipment are role models for the students. One of the problems for schools with ICT equipment is that often pupils have more up-to-date hardware at home. With books it is the opposite: school usually has a better range than home could possibly provide. Do not use tatty books; mend them or ask if they can be disposed of. Pencils should be sharp; carry a pencil sharpener and spare pens. Much time can be wasted on these little things. Your care and use of tools safely and appropriately sets an example. Even small children can and should clear up after themselves, and you should leave time for this in your session.

If you are using audio visual equipment such as a tape recorder, showing a video, or using a software programme on a computer, do make sure it all works before the lesson, and know where to go for technical help or spare bits when necessary. In some schools the TAs themselves are the organisers and technical help for all things electrical. Familiarise yourself with how an overhead projector works, and practise cleaning a whiteboard without the pupils present.

Active learning – intervention and non-intervention

Learning should be an active exercise where possible. Factual knowledge is more easily understood and learned where we practise its use or application. Literacy and numeracy can be extended by linking activities to pupils' particular hobbies or interests.

Pupils find active approaches stimulating as well as useful. Making a game of spellings, working as a group, or doing an investigation requires pupils to be active physically as well as mentally. Pupils get different insights from taking part, observing one another and talking things over with you and amongst themselves. Directing a group of active learners takes skill and practice, and the approach takes time and resources. It has to be set against the demands of the timetable and the effectiveness of other methods. A balance is needed and this will be set by the teacher for the whole lesson. But you may be able to adjust how you present some materials, to make them more interactive and fun.

It is equally important to recognise when pupils need to be left on their own to pursue a certain activity. Writing a poem or essay, or recalling an event, may need absolute quiet, even a table facing a wall. In libraries, tables set out for study sometimes have partitions between them to isolate the students from one another.

When a group or an individual is doing a task, the skill of the TA is to know when to intervene and when to stand back, and how to offer help when requested. You are not there to do the task for the pupil, however small. Give encouragement by doing an example. In art or craft work, have a piece of sewing or draw on your piece of paper, showing how it might be done. When asked for spelling, always get the pupils to try first or to use a dictionary, or even to tell you what the initial sound is. They need to develop their skills and gain confidence in their own ability.

Working with groups

We have seen (Chapter 4) that learners need language and social interaction to aid them. Group work can fulfil these needs, but there is much more to it than sitting them round a table and letting them do their own thing.

Group work means working together as a group, and children will need help in how to do this. Nowadays, social interaction in families is much less than it was, and they may need some practice in interacting with one another purposefully.

You will need to think carefully about the following points:

- How will the seating be organised – in a circle or round a table?
- When may the pupils speak?
- How can everyone be encouraged to contribute?
- How will you ensure they understand what kind of outcome is required?
- How will you bring out the reluctant pupil, cope with the domineering one, and eventually show the group how to do this for themselves?

The group may need a leader and a scribe, and these will need to know what their roles are. Specific subjects may have particular requirements: a craft model may need a variety of skills and tools; a science experiment will need further rules of safety; a cooking project will have to follow hygiene procedures; a debate can be set up as two opposing sides. Your role may be to monitor and report back to the teacher how the group worked and what was achieved. Be sure to time the exercise to allow for summing up, and for clearing up.

Circle time can be formally set up with only those holding a particular artefact being able to speak. The outcome may merely be to allow everyone to voice an opinion. Circle time, if used to explore feelings, needs trained people to lead it, as it could provoke unexpected or disturbing reactions from vulnerable pupils. Discuss this with your mentor and line manager, and never do circle time on your own unless you have the appropriate skills.

Occasionally, TAs are asked to take a whole class. Think carefully before you do this. Keeping a large group on task takes a great deal of skill, and is a huge responsibility. Legally, any adult can stand in front of a class *in an emergency*, provided they do not teach. As we have seen, the definition of teaching is difficult in itself. Thus if the qualified teacher is taken ill, you can hold the fort for a short time until another qualified teacher arrives to take the class. However, if the qualified teacher is present in the room, or sufficiently close to still be called 'in charge' of the class, you may take the large group. This sort of situation often happens with younger pupils, when you read a story or sing with a large group while the teacher does something special with a small group or an individual. With older children the teacher may set a task for the larger group to get on with, leaving you to ensure they carry it out, while he or she deals with something specialised within call. This is an appropriate use of your talents and their expertise. But you are not a qualified teacher and may not take on a teacher's responsibilities in their absence, however well you know the pupils. You may not be paid properly to take a class, nor might you be properly insured. Even student teachers have to have a qualified teacher present for lessons like PE. It is also the area where, rightly, qualified teachers get worried about being 'done out of a job'.

Practical work

Practical work brings together many of the above skills: working with a group, organising resources or equipment, explaining, giving tuition, questioning and observing. The pupils will be active, mobile and as independent as possible. Health and safety procedures must be paramount. ASE (1996; 2001) have produced useful guidance in this. There may be a copy of their documents in the staffroom. Ask the head of science or the science co-ordinator to check what you intend, if they have not already given you full instructions.

Pupils have to be taught to use tools correctly and the tools should be of good quality. Even very small children, supervised, are safer with good scissors than blunt ones. But they need to be shown how to carry them safely, and to cut out pieces of paper or fabric from the edge and not the middle. Measuring instruments should be used correctly. Make sure you know yourself what to do and what level of accuracy is required. Are you using millimetres or centimetres? Do you know how to read liquid measures using the meniscus correctly? Do you know where all the tools go when you have finished, so that you can direct the pupils to clean them and put them away ready for the next group?

Pupils may need help in making notes; it is different from writing full sentences. They may need advice on how to make a drawing of what they set up. Clarify with the teacher what is the real purpose of the task to be done, and make the pupils aware of it. Is it the answer to 'find out what happens when…' or 'how many do you need to…'? Or is the objective to give them experience of certain equipment, or find a way to test?

In art, the pupil may put emphasis on the end product, and whether or not they can achieve what is required; but the teacher's objective may be to explore a variety of media, to find their potential for some other purpose entirely. Self-esteem in artistic pursuits can so easily be dented by an over-emphasis on product too early.

Observing and listening

Always have part of an ear to what the teacher is doing. Always stop when the teacher addresses the class as a whole, and ensure your group or individual charge listen. A non-verbal gesture of a finger on your lips, or even a look, will help.

Eighty per cent of time in school can be spent on what the teacher or TA gives out, and only twenty per cent spent on pupils actively participating. Again, one of the opportunities for a TA working with a small group is to recognise when to talk and when to listen. You can even talk about listening with the older pupils – how you can all do it.

Pupils appreciate feedback on how they are getting on, but be clear about the expectations of the teacher, so that you do not set too low or too high a standard. On the whole it is better to stretch a pupil, setting a higher rather than a lower target, so long as they do not lose confidence or give up attempting what they see as the impossible. Check with the teacher involved.

Combining skills – multi-tasking

Another observable trait of teachers and TAs is their ability to multi-task. This, along with your relative mobility, means you become a 'flexible friend' to the classroom. You can be a 'gofer' in times of emergency, a shoulder for a child to cry on, anything an extra pair of hands can do. You can be a go-between for a slower or shyer child, or calm a trouble spot where and when it occurs. Because you work with small groups or individuals, you can take account of individual needs in a way the teacher of the large group cannot. You can wait longer for answers, or check progress more frequently.

Try to maintain a balance between intervening and chivvying to get tasks completed. Allow pupils time and space to complete tasks on their own. It is a hard skill to achieve, but is worth every minute you spend trying. If you are observed working in the classroom for appraisal ask the observer to watch particularly for this balance in yourself, so that you know how you are doing.

Review: feedback and reflection

Sometimes schools are not able to pay TAs for time to give feedback to the teacher out of pupil contact time. Fortunately, TAs and teachers find ways and means. Using unpaid time cannot be recommended practice. Informal times like tea breaks are really helpful and their impact should not be underestimated. Staffroom discussion of children's progress is a vital avenue of communication at all levels in school. In most schools now, TAs and other support staff are recognised as full members of the staffroom. You make a real contribution to the life and climate of the school.

Paper methods have been devised in some schools. The planning exercise book or sheets are used for you to record what happened, or who did what, or how well any particular pupil managed.

As you become experienced in watching children and young people at work, and more familiar with the curriculum, you will be able to make better judgements, not only about how they are doing but what the next step might be. All the observation protocols made in Chapter 4 apply here in terms of confidentiality and care of any documents you complete at school. Also, as you become experienced, your help may be enlisted by the teacher to do some more formal assessments. Doing these will give you an insight into what you can look out for while doing your own work, to feed back to the teacher.

Increasing your own competence

Get into the habit of reflecting after the lesson on what happened. You can do this as you go home, in the bath, or wherever you do your thinking. All good teachers do this. It is one of the reasons teaching is so demanding – the job goes on after you have left the site. If you become serious about your professional development you may even start keeping a simple reflective diary. You do not need to make a daily entry, just note a particular thing that happened and what you felt or thought about it. Keep this document confidential since you are writing about other people and other people's children.

How did I do?

Some key questions you could ask yourself:

- What is the purpose of what I am doing? What are the pupils to learn?
- Were they interested?
- Did I notice all of the ones for whom I was responsible?
- Did I do different things at different times? Did I instruct and explain appropriately?
- What questions did I use? Who answered?
- Was I confident, relaxed, supportive, encouraging?
- Did I smile or shout? Did I talk too much?
- Did I show respect?
- Were the resources good, or just adequate? Can I improve on them?
- What would I do differently, given the same circumstances, to make it better?
- Did I know enough about the subject, or is there some more I should find out?

If you get used to asking yourself some of the questions in the box, even informally, you will find it easier to be observed and have someone else comment in these areas. It may help you decide which area you would like to improve on and thus where the focus of any appraisal observation might be.

Relationships with the teacher

We have discussed the importance of establishing boundaries with the teacher with whom you are working. If there is a problem, confide in your mentor or line manager. You cannot sort out the more difficult issues; they must be sorted out by the school. The next chapter deals with the context of the school.

**Questions to ask before going into a different
teacher's classroom**

What do you particularly want me to do?

What do I do if a pupil in your room asks to go to the toilet?

Can I write in pupils' books?

What contact with parents or carers do you expect of the TA?

Do you want me to attend consultation evenings?

Do I take part in SEN reviews?

Can I do anything at the request of a parent such as change a
child's reading book or search for lost equipment?

Can I tidy the rooms? Your desks? The resources area?

Is there anything you do not want me to do?

Chapter 6

Being part of the school team

TAs are part of the classroom partnership and of the whole school team. School policies affect you and you should be included in all the appraisal and performance pay strategies, and in all the staff training relevant to the pupils or curriculum with which you are involved. Having rights always brings with it responsibilities, so you must be prepared to play your part as a member of the team. You may be employed on a part-time basis but nowadays part-timers have equal opportunities for pensions (sometimes called superannuation), sick pay and holiday with respect to the time they work. Many teachers work part time too.

In order to play your part in the team and feel supported by the organisation and the rest of the staff you need to understand something of the way in which schools work, and to keep yourself up-to-date and contribute where you can.

Most of what is written in this chapter refers to state schools. Independent schools may well have different ways of organising themselves. The school building will have little effect on the structure and systems, which are how the school works. Many schools still operate very effectively in old buildings; there are open plan schools where walls have been built and Victorian buildings where walls have been knocked down; some schools are opened in purpose built, environmentally friendly buildings. All have their joys and drawbacks. What makes a school an effective and pleasant place to be in are the people who work in the building. This chapter will look more closely at the organisation within the building and the ways in which people operate.

Structures and systems

Getting to know who is who

You will have met several teachers, have a designated line manager, and have identified the SENCO. The head teacher may or may not have been part of your appointment process, but you should be aware who that person is. If you do not have a copy of a staff file you could try to complete the checklist in the box. You may need help, and you will not be able to do it all at once.

Who does what in your school?

Photocopy this sheet and add in the names on it

Responsibility	Teacher	Governor	Other adult
Head teacher			
Deputy head(s)			
Who is responsible for:			
English			
Mathematics			
Science			
ICT			
Other subjects with which you might be connected:			
Children with SEN – the SENCO			
Assessment or examinations			
Health and Safety			
Child protection issues – the named person			
Various union reps			
Careers			
Liaison with other schools			
Liaison with outside agencies			
The office			
The cleaning			
The site management			
The teaching assistant team			
The kitchen			
First aid			
Other:			

The same names may appear in many different boxes if your school is small, as people have to double up on the jobs. As you ask, you will begin to find out what those jobs involve, and how they affect you. It is useful to make contact with the caretaker early on, so that when you want help with spilt paint, need bin bags, or find a leak, you know whom to contact. You also need to identify the people responsible for the curriculum areas in which you will be working so that you know how to get resources and answers to your questions.

Just as you are responsible to a line manager, so each person is responsible to someone 'above' them. The school staff structure can look like a pyramid with the head teacher at the top. The head teacher has responsibility for running the school, but that responsibility is only delegated to the head by the Governing Body. It is worth finding out their names (they may have their photographs in the foyer) and having a look at their Annual Report to parents. Governors do not have responsibilities in the same way as staff, as they have to act as a body, but they often have separate specialities, separate committees to discuss things about the school. Support staff have to elect a representative to speak on their behalf to the Governing Body, as necessary. The representative should know where minutes of meetings of the Governing Body are kept, and what the governors' views are of the TAs in your school. You could add this person's name to your checklist box.

The head may or may not have an official deputy, but someone will be appointed to deputise in their absence. They would then take responsibility for the day-to-day running, in case of emergency. You should know who this person is. Communication systems vary in schools. Some have various forms of daily and weekly diaries. There may be a notice board in the staffroom to ensure this communication works.

Your line manager may or may not be part of a senior manager team. In secondary schools, the subject leaders are called departmental heads. Some staff take cross-curricular leadership roles, as year group or Key Stage leader, and they may lead in planning and assessment strategies for a group of teachers. You may be slotted into any one of these managerial teams. They often have their own systems and structures, meetings and resources areas. Teachers in larger schools get extra salary points for responsibility, but in smaller schools these points are correspondingly fewer. Ask about it. Extra responsibility may involve a pastoral role such as looking after staff development, pupil care, parent liaison or SEN; or it may cover organisational matters like timetabling, display or an environmental area or library. Sometimes some of these responsibilities may be taken on by TAs.

In schools for children of 11 and older, teachers may have a pastoral or tutorial responsibility for a year group class, but will have been appointed for their subject expertise. All teachers now have to have a degree in a NC subject. The plan is that in secondary schools you teach those subjects in which you have most expertise. Unfortunately it does not always work like that, and there are mismatches. Some subjects are less popular than others. Modern languages and religious education teachers are scarce, as are mathematics and physics teachers. Teachers may also have to cover for absent colleagues who teach a different subject. However the principle remains that usually teachers in secondary schools are directed to teach their specialist subjects across several age ranges, and so teach many more children, often up to 200 a week. Primary teachers usually have a class which they teach for most subjects and children spend most of the day with the one adult. This makes a significant difference to the way in which you operate.

Your job description

You should have been given a job description when you started, and so it should be clear to you what you have to do. In the beginning it is unlikely that you will have too many different things to do, but the nature of the job is to support and assist where you can. If you have particular responsibilities these should be clearly laid out for you. As you get settled, you may be asked to do something different, or work in a different place, with different people. Or you may begin to offer to do other things. Keep a note of these so that when your job description is reviewed (which it should be at least annually), you can have the new tasks written into a revised version. Your professional portfolio would be a good place for any notes you want to keep. There are many examples of job descriptions published now: see the *Good Practice Guide* (DfEE 2000b p. 18) and the books by Lorenz (1998 pp. 70–3) and Fox (1998 pp. 80, 81).

Your pay and contract

Your school has a name, which will give some indication of how it is governed or run. It might be a church school and these can be run differently. The status of the school affects the way it is funded, which in turn may affect how and what you are paid. Foundation schools are funded directly from central government, and will be the employer. All other state schools determine salaries and contracts but the Local Education Authority is the employer, and usually the paymaster: that is, they send out the pay cheques.

Finding your way about

> **Where do things happen?**
> Get your map of the classrooms, and put a name to each area. Then, if you have an accident in any of them, want to know anything about the area, or would like to borrow something from them, you will know to whom to go.

School buildings are confusing. Changes in the way pupils are taught have brought changes to the use of areas. More class teaching means some schools have put up walls in previously open plan areas. The developments of ICT have meant computer suites becoming as common as libraries. You need to know your own school circumstances. Classes are not necessarily organised in year groups, or even in Key Stages. It depends on the numbers of children in the school, the accommodation, and the management decisions of the school. Ask your teacher/mentor to explain the circumstances of decisions made in your own school.

The locality and how it affects the school and your job

Local people from the surrounding community can get involved in the life of the school. They may contribute to the resources. Some businesses may visit or even exchange staff, or they may encourage visits to their premises. Other local services like the police or the health service may have representatives who make regular visits to the school. The vicar, minister, rabbi, imam, or other religious people may be seen at assembly or in the classrooms of any school, not just those with a religious title in their name. Some schools visit their local place of worship regularly and others never. All these contacts add a dimension to the school.

A school is made up of staff and pupils, but increasingly parents and governors have roles to play. Governors usually have a rota for visiting the school so that they can get to know it. If they have the responsibility for the school, they have to know how it looks on a day-to-day basis. Do talk with your teacher/mentor about the Governing Body in your school, who is on it and why, and see what interests they have in the locality.

You may have been a parent working as a volunteer. There will be a number working in the school. Parents are often consulted on matters like school uniform, or the best way of relaying news of a pupil's progress. They run associations, usually to raise money for the school. As a TA you may be asked to liaise with particular parents about their children who have special needs, but usually the teacher deals directly with them on all curriculum matters. Be careful not to be drawn in by parents who ask you about their child's progress or behaviour at school. Refer them to the teacher concerned. You may be asked to join the teacher or the SENCO when reviews take place of pupils with SEN, particularly if you are closely associated with that pupil. The teacher concerned will advise you about your role in that meeting.

At some time you will come into contact with visiting teachers or advisers. Most schools have a liaison person concerned with the teaching of special needs. Various specialists will then visit, depending on the needs of the pupils, for example, an occupational therapist, a physiotherapist or a speech therapist. If you are working with a pupil with a particular need, then you should be included when that specialist comes to the school. The teacher may even delegate dealing with that visitor to you. These specialists will understand thoroughly the condition concerning the pupil, but will not know so much about the way the pupil has to work in school; so your partnership with them can be very supportive for the pupil. If, for instance, your charge has a hearing impairment, it makes sense that you know how to operate the hearing aids, what to do if things go wrong, and when your pupil needs the aids the most, or can get along without them. It makes sense that you learn sign language if that is used. It makes sense that you spend time on the practical things and liaise with the teacher later. You may have useful suggestions to make to either the teacher or the therapist. It will be a professional partnership.

Curriculum and teaching policies

Policies

It is for the school to interpret how the NC and other activities are carried out in the school. The governors are responsible for seeing that this is done, and the teachers have to do it. You help in this process. Sometimes it is difficult for a newcomer to pick up how to go about things. But much more is made explicit now, and less is left to chance or intuition. Paperwork is used to record decisions and methods, and this is looked at in a school inspection. Not everything that happens in a school is set out in a written policy but more and more is, so that everyone can work in the same way. Schools will have a **curriculum policy**, laying out how and what is taught; and it is recommended that they have a **teaching and learning policy** to describe how teaching is to be done and what learning objectives are to be reached. Your role should be spelt out in these since you help 'deliver' the curriculum and assist the teaching and learning.

Other policies

You might like to look at some of the other policies with your teacher/mentor. Select a few that you think will be relevant to you and start there. First, find out where all the policies are kept. Then, when an interest or issue arises, you can go and look it up. The policies mentioned in the sections below – Health and Safety, Confidentiality, Child Protection, and Behaviour Management – are very relevant to your job: you should have your own copy of each of these. Try to take a look at English and Mathematics, as these come up in most other subjects, as does ICT. If you are supporting pupils with SEN, then the SEN policy may be helpful. At some point you should take a look at policies to do with pay and conditions of service, and any covering equal opportunities or inclusion, cultural diversity and anti-discrimination. For those of you supporting pupils whose home language is not English, there may be a policy to help you with that.

Health and safety

As an employee you have a responsibility to be aware of potential dangers and to know what to do if there is a problem. This covers obvious things like fire alarms, the security of the building and grounds, and what to do about a blocked toilet; it also includes access to classrooms or playgrounds, and the storage of packed lunches to avoid food risks. All schools have these Health and Safety policies and there will be staff with special responsibilities to ensure the health and safety of all people in the premises: pupils, staff and visitors. The main emphases are on reasonableness and risk assessment. Some school buildings are old and difficult to make secure or accessible for wheelchairs. Others have worries with alarms and one-way entry doors, and you will need to familiarise yourself with these. There is a checklist in the *Teaching Assistant File* (DfEE 2000a pp. 3.8 and 3.9 and DfES 2001a pp. 1.48–1.52).

Confidentiality in general

All members of staff, professionals and volunteers should maintain confidentiality about all that they see, hear or read while in school. You may wish a child received more attention at home, or was kept away from another child, but that cannot be said outside the professional dialogue with staff in the school. Likewise you should not comment about a child's progress – this is the teacher's job. Parents do approach TAs about their children, perhaps because they know you, or because you are less busy than the teachers. It is tempting to relay gossip to a friend, when you are dying to tell someone, so take great care.

Child protection

This is a sensitive and important area. It is hoped that all schools have written policies in this area and ensure that all staff are trained together, but it is not always the case. If it does not happen in your school, then suggest it.

Teachers and other school staff act *in loco parentis*. The Children Act applies to schools as well as the general population. The school policy should lay out clear guidelines for *all* staff on what to do if there is a suspicion of abuse, and on how to prevent allegations against staff themselves. There should be a designated Child Protection person whose name is known by all staff, who is trained in what to do and where to go if help is needed.

There are two main areas of sensitivity: recognising the signs of abuse; and behaving appropriately as a member of staff.

1. Signs of abuse

    You should be aware of the possible signs of abuse. These are not always physical. Abuse can also be mental, or emotional, or be the result of neglect. This is not the place to describe all the signs and symptoms of abuse. You need some training from the LEA Child Protection Officer (or whoever is responsible for it in your area). All children can have bruises from accidents or playing roughly. It is the type of bruise and where it is on the body that can be important. Do not be obsessive or inquisitive, but be vigilant – for instance when children change for PE, or are talking informally.

A child may reveal to you what has happened to them. You are particularly well placed for children to feel secure with you. You work in small groups or with individual pupils for periods of time and build up friendly relations. No school staff are trained to deal with children or families in detail, in child protection matters, but you all have a responsibility to recognise and report to people who are. Do not question a child in these circumstances, as you may ask leading questions; and never promise not to tell anyone. Listen carefully, sensitively, caringly, inwardly note what they say, and then tell the designated member of staff as soon as possible. Make a short written record afterwards, date it, and give it to this named member of staff. It is that person's responsibility to deal with it by informing Social Services or the police.

Incidents are rarely clear cut. If you have any doubts about what you have heard or seen, discuss it with the class teacher, your teacher/mentor, the designated teacher or the head. If you are involved further, be guided by the named person in the school. These people will understand about case conferences, child protection registers, and agencies who can support vulnerable children and their families. Be sure to maintain confidentiality with the staff concerned, in all these proceedings.

2. Appropriate staff behaviour

The other area where you can be involved in child protection issues is when you are dealing with children in intimate situations. This may happen when dealing with pupils with physical disabilities, or very young children who have toileting accidents. Usually the parents know what the school policy is, whether school staff can clean children up after toilet accidents or change underclothes. TAs are sometimes asked to work in pairs when these events occur.

Always comfort unhappy children, but do it in public not privately. Never put yourself into a situation which could lead to unjustified accusation. Pupils need sometimes to see school as a haven, a place of safety and security which they may not otherwise have. Always be aware of, and respond to, troubled children, but recognise how to do this appropriately. Do not single them out for attention; it is better for them to come to you.

Another aspect of this policy can arise when dealing with difficult pupils. Touching pupils, let alone restraining pupils, can get you into difficulties with parents, and even the law. The pupils concerned are usually particularly volatile, liable to act up, or react unnecessarily to being told how to behave. Do make sure you know the school policy on restraint and, if possible, get appropriate training in this area. You should not be put in a difficult position with a pupil swearing in your face, being aggressive or dangerous to others in your early days in the school. If problems arise, make sure you talk immediately to your line manager. Most LEAs have specialists in this area who can help.

Discipline and behaviour management

There are books dealing solely with this issue (Hook and Vass 2000; Fox 2001), and so this book will not deal with it at length. One of the keys to managing pupils' behaviour is having all staff using a consistent way of dealing with whatever happens. There is no point your telling a pupil off for what you consider is inappropriate or unacceptable language or behaviour, if a teacher considers it acceptable. Likewise, if you are slacker than the teachers are, the pupils will behave badly with you and try to get away with things. Find out what rewards and sanctions you can use, and who to appeal to or send a pupil to if there is an incident you cannot deal with.

Being part of a team

As part of a team, you share concerns. This means you should:

- be caring and responsible;
- treat pupils and adults with respect;
- always reflect that there is a distinction between a pupil's behaviour and the pupil themselves (i.e. it is the behaviour that is bad, not the pupil);
- be honest and tolerant;
- control your temper and emotions;
- be a professional.

A key area to consider is relationships. Test this by asking yourself the questions in the box. If any of your answers are unsatisfactory, is there anything you can do about it?

Questions about relationships in school

Is the school a happy place?

Are all staff consulted and involved in decision making in school?

How are pupils asked their opinions?

Can their views be used?

Are the children confident and relaxed when talking to staff?

Are differences of opinions, conflicts, etc. discussed openly in classrooms? the staffroom?

Do all staff feel valued members of the school?

How welcome do parents feel in the school?

How welcome do governors feel in the school?
Does the school reach out to those sections of the community/parents which are less involved in school?
What opportunities are there for parents and the school to share their hopes and expectations?
How accessible is the head teacher to the pupils, the staff and the parents?
How accessible are staff to children, parents and governors?
How do we show that the opinions and help and support of parents and/or governors are valued?
What opportunities are there for the pupils to link with the community?
Is there mutual respect?

Equal opportunities policy

Another area which affects the climate of the school is whether it provides equal opportunities for all. This does not mean equal provision. It means creating provision so that all have an equal opportunity to reach their potential. It means considering how gender affects the way we behave towards one another. Gender barriers can be created unintentionally by always asking boys to move furniture or girls to clear up, or having pupils line up in boys' and girls' lines.

You can also create opportunities for those of a different race or culture to contribute to the richness of school life. Show interest in them. Ask what hobbies they have got, what they do at the weekend, where they went for holidays. This will help you build up a relationship, and will also help others in the group to appreciate the variety of lifestyles. Encourage talk about clothes, ask to see photographs or pieces of material: these can range from football shirts to saris.

Equal opportunities involves recognising achievement in academic and non-academic fields. You can play your part by promoting high standards for all, and recognising those strategies that promote self-esteem, prevent bullying, and help pupils value one another.

The School Development Plan

One key document of a school, though not really a policy, is the School Development Plan (SDP). This is now sometimes referred to as the School Improvement Plan, as its main intention is to develop systems to create change for the better. The SDP is the business plan for the organisation called school. It should have strategic and long term ideas of where the school wants to be in two or three years' time, and a more detailed plan of what is going to happen in the year ahead. It will take into account the aims of the school, and the vision of the governors for the school. It has to take account of any legally imposed or recommended national initiatives. It will have looked at the strengths and weaknesses of the school, in order to consider what changes need to be made, and what can be built on.

It sets out the costs of the improvements for the year, and who will be responsible for them, so it should include something about the role of TAs. Thus, some of the changes planned will affect you. Ask your mentor to show you any relevant bits. Since staff are included in the plan, they should also be consulted about how well last year's plan worked for them, and what could be included for the future. It is your responsibility to be as well informed as you can be, if you want to play a part in these team consultations.

Professional development for all

Some schools have the Investors in People (IiP) award or are working towards Investors in People status for their schools. If you do not know, ask your mentor about it. The Investors in People standard has four main principles.

> An Investor in People:
> - is fully committed to developing its people in order to achieve its aims and objectives;
> - is clear about its aims and its objectives and what its people need to do to achieve them;
> - develops its people effectively in order to improve its performance;
> - understands the impact of its investment in people on its performance. (Investors in People and DfEE 2000)

While such statements accept that overall the responsibility for 'the people' in the organisation lies with the senior management, each person has to do their bit. Thus, if you are consulted, respond honestly. Read the School Development Plan where it relates to your work. Ensure you get a copy of the Annual Report to parents. Go to the Annual Meeting. Find out who the support staff governor is. TAs have been known to offer good ideas about streamlining timetables or ICT processed feedback systems which were taken up by their line managers and the teachers.

You are responsible for your own learning and professional development, for finding out more about the job and your performance, and acting on suggestions. This is taking personal responsibility for fulfilling your job description appropriately. In the past, TAs were often the forgotten members of the school team, invisible, coming and going when others were occupied elsewhere. You are now recognised as important partners in the learning and teaching process. Your induction procedures should ensure you have a much greater understanding of what the school is about and how it works. If you don't know – ask! Polite questions at convenient times will help you and enable you to be part of the whole.

When you take part in staff meetings, in-service education for teachers (INSET) and the staffroom every day, listen to and talk with the teachers; and do some planning with them. It is important that you do make time for this. It is only by developing a joint understanding that you will meet the needs of the pupils. Being part of a team has benefits in term of friendships for you but you can also add humour and maybe challenge to the staff team. You have, by definition, less responsibility and paperwork, and often provide light relief or even the shoulder to cry on for overstretched, harassed teachers. Good relationships with pupils and other staff not only make the school a better place to work in but also make it possible to raise difficult, subtle and confidential issues essential to work.

Your school

To conclude, think about the following list of characteristics of an effective school. It was drawn up after a large research project in some London schools called *School Matters* (Mortimore *et al.* 1988). The project identified some key characteristics of successful schools, which were:

- leadership – staff selection, consensus and unity of purpose, professionalism and understanding;
- shared vision and goals;
- attractive and orderly environment with self-managing classrooms, reflecting positive ethos;
- concentration on teaching and learning – monitoring of effective time spent;
- purposeful, well-organised teaching, clear pace, structure, and objectives reflected in preparation, effective questioning strategies;
- high expectations and self-esteem of teachers, pupils and parents;
- positive reinforcement, clear feedback, rewards and disciplinary procedures;
- monitoring of progress, focusing on goals, informing planning and teaching;
- pupil rights and responsibilities enabling pupil participation, raising self-esteem and independent learning;
- home–school partnerships fostering support and making demands;
- senior managers and teachers, as well as students continue to be learners.

(Sammons, Hillman and Mortimore 1995)

Can you see how you can be part of such a school? Another similar list which you can discuss with your mentor is derived from the principles of the International School Effectiveness and Improvement Centre. They are that:

- all children can learn, albeit in different ways at different rates;
- individual schools can make a substantial difference to the development, progress and achievement of pupils;
- effective schools add value to pupils' lives;
- effective schools focus on a range of learning outcomes, including academic, practical, creative, personal and social;
- schools improve most by focusing on learning and teaching, while also addressing their culture and internal conditions;
- partnership is a fundamental element of successful school improvement;
- intervention work needs to be based on appropriate research findings.

(Sammons 1999 p. 340)

If you find these lists too daunting try finding an analogy from the box.

Try to draw your school

No, not a scenic view, but an analogy.

Is it like a garden centre?
   Having a manager and staff, customers and a product
   But the products are living things, all different with differing needs
   There are fertilisers and pest controllers
   And…

Or is it a stage?
   With performers and an audience
   A producer and backstage staff
   A script writer and critics
   Practice makes perfect…
   It repeats the same thing day in and day out – or does it?…

Or a ship?
   With a captain and crew, passengers of various kinds
   In a rough sea and a calm one
   Needing fuel and equipment, which could be of varying ages
   Does it navigate by the stars or with a compass…?

Or…?

Chapter 7

Outside support and influences

Schools come under national government legislation. All have to work within the framework of the National Curriculum as well as employment, health and safety laws and the Children Act. These laws vary in the different countries making up the UK, but they largely provide for funding arrangements, curriculum and examination regulations, and laws regulating the structure and maintenance of the learning environment. There is plenty of written guidance to help schools operate within these frameworks. Most of these documents are published by the government department responsible for education, or other approved organisations.

A legal framework

The government department for education has been through several name changes, which is slightly confusing. Thus, the Department of Education and Science (DES) replaced the Ministry of Education in 1964, only to become amalgamated with Employment to become the Department for Education and Employment (DfEE) in the 1990s. That became the Department for Education and Skills (DfES) after the 2001 election. Three separate organisations which also formulate policy affecting schools in England and Wales are:

1. The **Qualifications and Curriculum Authority** (QCA) oversees the processes of examinations and qualifications and came into being from the amalgamation of the Schools Curriculum and Assessment Authority (SCAA) and the National Council for Vocational Qualifications (NCVQ). This means that all qualifications, including the new TA ones (see Chapter 8), are passing through QCA's hands. There they will be checked against the new National Occupational Standards (LGNTO 2001) for TAs. The new NVQs for TAs will be drawn up by the Examination Boards, and then checked by QCA.

2. The **Office for Standards in Education** (Ofsted) oversees school inspection. You will certainly come into contact with a team from Ofsted at some point as a TA when the school in which you work is inspected. The team will come from a contractor, but Ofsted sets the standards and monitors the teams. Ofsted staff also include Her Majesty's Inspectorate (HMI), who visit schools from time to time.

3. The **Teacher Training Agency** (TTA) determines the nature and standards for teacher training. You may want to look at their documents if you ever consider becoming a qualified teacher.

Relevant Acts that affect education

All schools come under the Children Act and school staff act *in loco parentis*. This affects things like the child protection guidelines on procedures for all staff.

All schools have to conform to the relevant parts of the Health and Safety laws. Among other things, this entails having written policies, fire precautions and kitchens which conform to hygiene regulations. Fire officers and other health and safety inspectors will visit the school to check these from time to time.

Industrial legislation includes things like the Factory Acts and employment law, and covers things like your use of refreshment and toilet areas and a right to equal pay for equal work. Schools are sometimes anomalies in these acts; for instance, the Act requires a qualified first-aider for 50 or more staff in an establishment. A school can have fewer than this number of staff, but maybe 200 children, and are not legally required to have a certified first-aider. In practice, most will have one.

Local legislation can be involved in things like planning permissions and by-laws concerning trespass or rights of way.

Copyright laws govern tape and video recording, photocopying and faxing. Some of these tasks may be part of your job. Usually the school will post extracts from the law next to the photocopier, and you may have to fill in some sort of logbook if you copy material from textbooks. Ask the school administrative staff if you are worried. Assistants support children using ICT, but in some schools they are also becoming the ICT technicians: Most schools are now connected to the Internet, but hopefully they will have installed 'fire walls' to protect the pupils from coming into contact with pornography or other inappropriate sites or chat rooms. If in doubt, check with someone.

Special Educational Needs

This is an area that is covered with a great deal of statutory provision (i.e. laws). These are designed to get funding and help to those pupils who have special needs. This is a large area and many whole books are devoted to it. The draft document with all the recent legislation is the SEN *Code of Practice* (DfEE 2000c). There may be a copy in the staffroom. It governs all the recommendations about 'statements', IEPs, and the role of the SENCO, and talks much more about inclusion. SEN pupils used to be labelled by their deficiencies or handicap. Now they are described by their needs.

The area of special needs can seem bureaucratic, cumbersome and expensive to administer, with different LEAs interpreting the act in different ways. Some authorities have established teams of assistants; others provide support through peripatetic special needs teachers; schools in other authorities are delegated funding earmarked for SEN. As a TA for SEN, your salary may come out of funding earmarked for those pupils who have a special need.

The current main aim in SEN is to promote inclusion: this means that all pupils should be educated together where possible, with appropriate support for those who have a special need. The principles of inclusion are well described in the early pages of the National Curriculum (DfEE 1999a; 1999b pp. 32–9). Eventually the label SEN will go and SENCOs will become Inclusion Co-ordinators.

The role of a Local Education Authority (LEA)

The government policy of Local Management of Schools (LMS), introduced in the late 1990s, means that much power has been transferred from LEAs to schools. Budgets were devolved to the schools, which became responsible for their own financial management and, in some cases, employment of staff. The LEA role has become more strategic and advisory: it monitors, challenges and supports schools. Some LEAs retain advisers to help improve the performance of schools, particularly those having difficulties. In addition to SEN services (see preceding section), LEAs usually offer some form of admissions and/or pupil services and personnel services. Library services, music and adult education may still be the responsibility of the LEA while services such as school meals and cleaning, planning and building surveyors may be contracted out to the private sector.

Some LEAs have special TA advisers, who organise courses, encourage networking, and recommend local qualifications and career pathways. Find out from your mentor or directly from your LEA what is going on for TAs in your area. There are enormous benefits from meeting colleagues from other schools and sharing ideas, and from learning more about children and young people, about the job and about the latest things to help teaching and learning. If there is nothing orgainsed, ask your line manager if you could visit a TA in a neighbouring school, or host an after school visit from TAs working nearby.

National accountability – tests

While most teachers see the NC as a good thing, and parents find it helpful to know what schools should be teaching, and what standard their children ought to be able to achieve, with it came a whole lot of systems for assessing children. You are bound to get involved with these. You may be asked to sit with a pupil to read the test paper to them, or practise bits ready for the tests. The externally set tests are called SATs (Standard Assessment Tests or Tasks) or examinations designed by the examination boards.

There are obvious problems with tests. Teachers may end up teaching to the tests and not to the whole NC. Tests do not show all that a pupil is capable of. Nor can tests be used for all parts of the curriculum. Practical investigational work of science in notoriously difficult to test. Many factors affect the results of a test: the time of the year, the intake date, the child's birthday position in the year, a change of school. GCSEs are not suitable for the whole ability range, and yet the newer vocational qualifications are less recognised by industry or businesses. Pupils themselves – particularly students aged 16 to 18 – are complaining about the current number of tests and examinations.

The collection of numerical data about pupils has made a big impact on schools. You may be asked to type into a database some of the data from the testing processes. New analysis systems have enabled pupils' progress to be tracked in a much more effective way than ever before. Trends, like whether girls or boys are doing better or worse, can be picked out. Along with this has come the idea of predicting what children should achieve and watching whether it happens. It can lead to setting targets for them which are higher than the prediction, and then aiming to fulfil the targets by increasing the teaching or support mechanisms for a particular child. You may be used in some of the classes to give an extra boost. Additional Literacy Support (ALS) materials (DfEE 1999d) were originally designed for those who had certain patterns of results in their tests. The target setting process has been really successful in raising expectations of what children can achieve in primary schools. Now secondary schools, at Key Stage 3, are having to look more closely at what they can do to build on the success.

National accountability – inspection and Ofsted

At some point in your career you will be part of an inspection. The purpose of an inspection is to form an outside opinion on the strengths and weaknesses of the school. There are long and short inspections. The short ones are for schools that have been inspected recently or very successfully and may only need a further check. The inspection team depend a lot on the school's documents and data on short inspections, and only observe a few lessons. On a long inspection, the team will spend at least 60 to 70 per cent their time in classrooms, so they are likely to watch you at work.

One of the better things about inspection is that the criteria the inspectors use is all published and available. It is call the Framework for Inspection and there are different ones for primary, secondary and special schools. Your school will already have been inspected at least once and all the reports are published in full on the Internet, on the Ofsted website. If you can locate it, and you have your own system, you can download it in minutes and print it off. Libraries will have copies and so will the school. They are long and difficult to read, but certain areas will relate to your work and will give you an understanding of your place in an inspection.

The Ofsted schedule for inspection covers the following areas, and the reports are written under these headings:

Context and overview
1. What sort of school is it?

Outcomes
2. How high are standards?
2.1 The school's results and pupils' achievements
2.2 Pupils' attitudes, values and personal developments

Quality of provision
3. How well are pupils taught?
4. How good are the curricular and other opportunities offered to pupils?
5. How well does the school care for its pupils?
6. How well does the school work in partnership with parents?

Efficiency and effectiveness of management
7. How well is the school led and managed?

Issues for the school
8. What should the school do to improve further? (Ofsted 1999 p. 6)

When the whole school is inspected, the main burden falls on classroom observation and the teacher, but the role of teaching assistants does not go unnoticed. Under section 3, the teaching section, meeting the needs of SEN pupils is listed, so the use of TAs in supporting these pupils may be commented on. It is rare, but not unknown, that an inspector completes a 'teaching' judgement form on a TA. If they appear to be doing this, try to catch them and ask them to comment. They will not show you what they have written but may be able to talk with you about what they saw.

Under section 5, caring for pupils, are included welfare, safety and child protection issues. Again, your work in the medical room, or as part of the counselling team, may be observed and commented on in the report.

Under the leadership and management section, section 7, inspectors have to comment on staffing. If you look in the Framework you find for instance:

Inspectors must evaluate and report on … the adequacy of staffing, … highlighting strengths and weaknesses in different subjects and areas of the curriculum where they affect the quality of education provided and the educational standards achieved … In determining their judgements, inspectors should consider the extent to which the number, qualifications and experience of teachers and support staff match the demands of the curriculum.

(Ofsted 1999 p. 92)

Page 106 of the framework deals with the adequacy of both teachers and support staff. You may well be asked to meet an inspector as part of a TA team, to speak about what you do, how you are organised and supported in the school. This is not something to be nervous of. It is recognition that your role is important in affecting the teaching and learning of the pupils in the school. How you are led and managed is significant in how well you can do your job.

What next?

Already some of the examination boards are submitting their qualifications to QCA to check their alignment with emerging national standards. Within a year it should be possible to match all the existing diverse individual qualifications to the Framework. NVQs are being developed to match the National Occupational Standards. All this will result in an ability to define the role and qualifications of TAs more closely. Some LEAs have drawn up exemplar job descriptions and are suggesting pay scales for work levels. If you have not come across these yet, ask about them. Meanwhile, your own continuing personal, professional development is important, and is dealt with in the next chapter.

Chapter 8

Taking this further: developing yourself

Your aim should always be to become better at your job. Talk about it with colleagues and teachers. Share ideas and resources. As you become more confident you could become instrumental in forming or helping a local support group. These groups not only discuss matters of pay and conditions but also can provide a way of maintaining your professional development without necessarily seeking further qualifications. Local speakers and advisers can be invited to talk on specialist areas, or matters relating to school developments or social needs.

Keep your personal professional file up-to-date. Whichever direction you take, your achievements with supporting pupils' learning will go with you; your file carries the evidence. More schools are now arranging appraisals for all staff, not just teachers. All staff are entitled to have their jobs reviewed.

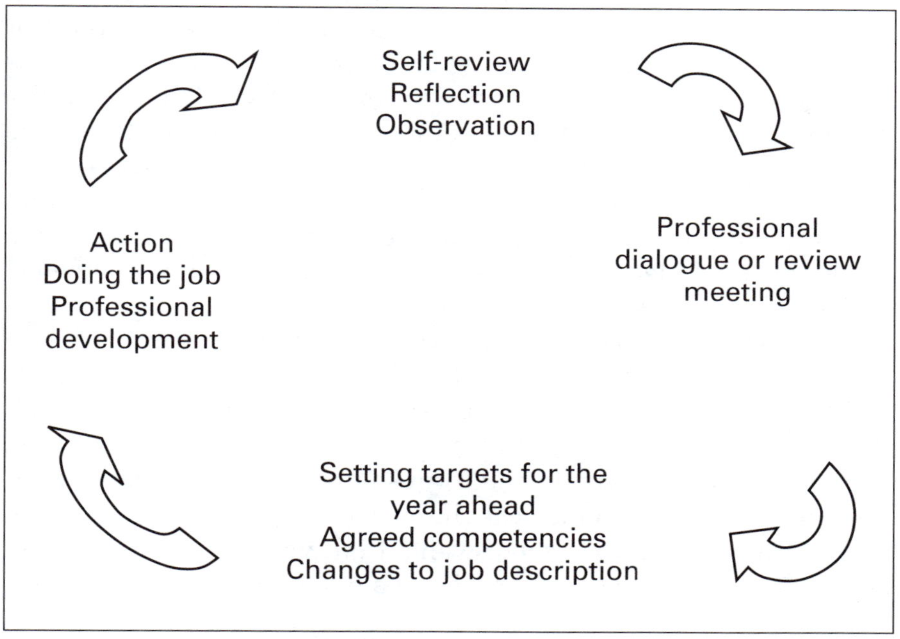

You and your job

Self-review
Reflection
Observation

Professional dialogue or review meeting

Action
Doing the job
Professional development

Setting targets for the year ahead
Agreed competencies
Changes to job description

Figure 8.1   The appraisal cycle

A job review has several constituents, shown in Figure 8.1, which repeat over the years. If you have been keeping notes in your file, you will go to any review meeting well prepared. You could make an extract from these notes to take with you or complete a checklist. Somebody may observe you at work and talk through with you what they see.

TA being observed by a teacher for an outside accredited course

This is a valuable opportunity for getting some constructive criticism. You can discuss what you would like observed beforehand – 'do I speak clearly enough?', 'do I explain sufficiently?', 'do I deal with particular children as well as I might?'.

The review proper is an occasion for professional dialogue. This is a formal opportunity to discuss your work with your mentor or line manager and to look at how it is developing. The purpose is to enhance professional development, to recognise and celebrate achievements, and to set targets for the future. This is the ideal time to discuss your ideas and needs. Make the most of having someone else just thinking of you!

A TA's work often changes from year to year, term to term, or even day to day if a new pupil with particularly challenging needs suddenly moves into the area. An annual review of your job description is therefore useful for you and your managers. Think about what you already do and form some idea, if possible, of what you might like to do in the year ahead. Your appraiser will also have some ideas of what the school wants from you. Both of these may entail you going on a course, or doing a bit of background reading.

Listing all the things that you do

How does this compare with your job description?

There are some notes for managers on appraisal in Lorenz (1998 pp. 86–9) with a useful self-review sheet. Another self-review sheet can be found in the *Teaching Assistant File* (DfEE 2000a pp. 4.3–4.7 and DfES 2001a 1.42–1.45). Self-review (see box) is something you do before you talk anything over with someone else. You can keep the results private or share them with your reviewer or appraiser.

Constituents of the self-review

(This is not something that can be completed in one go. Try it a bit at a time.)

List your:

- Successes and appreciation from others
- Job satisfaction and lack of it – fulfilling your existing job description
- Relationships with pupils, colleagues and others associated with the school
- Understanding of the learning process and special educational needs
- Teaching skills and contribution to the learning objectives of the teachers
- Relevant curriculum knowledge and understanding
- Contributions to pastoral and physical care and behaviour management
- Understanding of and contributions to school life
- Professional development opportunities taken: training, courses, meetings attended, personal study undertaken, in school or out of school
- Setting and achieving of any personal targets
- Areas for change, development or improvement – adjustments to job description, and career development issues or ideas.

There need to be some ground rules agreed between you and whoever is going to review your work. Talk with them informally beforehand and make sure you each know what you are going to do and achieve.

Ground rules for professional dialogues or appraisals

- Ownership
- What happens to any paperwork
- Confidentiality
- Honesty
- Outcomes contributing to the school's staff development plan
- Developmental status
- An action plan – the responsibility for which will lie with you, facilitated by others
- An understanding of the place of the dialogue in the processes of the school

How will the dialogue take place? It needs to be formally arranged, in quality time, but comfortable. There should be open dialogue, but all that is said should be confidential and in an atmosphere of trust.

After the interview has taken place, a recorded note of the targets should be given to the member of staff who is responsible for staff development and/or the head teacher. Governors need only know that the interview has taken place.

Study skills

Whatever you plan to do in the future – whether this is a job you intend to remain in or one step in a career plan – you will need to develop study skills if you want to be a really good TA.

Study skills include personal organisation systems, recording information, reflecting on what you are doing and sharing professional ideas. You can practise observing, note-taking, reading, writing essays or accounts, finding reference books and organising your time. Skills improve as you practise them. There are books on study skills, such as *The Good Study Guide* (Northledge 1990), which may help.

Personal organisers can be really helpful to start with. Include a timetable of your whole day, not just your school day. When do you eat, talk with your friends or family, relax, sleep? Try to build in some time just for you, even if it is only an hour a week. Try to have somewhere in your home to keep your school things – books, artefacts, your files and folders. If you start a training course you will probably need a whole shelf for the books and materials you collect. Find somewhere to study – to read or write undisturbed. TAs sometimes find themselves studying after everyone else has gone to bed, particularly if you have videos to watch as part of a course. It is worthwhile putting in some time and thought to these practical issues and discussing them with your family. This could save some arguments or heartache later. Begin gently: set yourself realistic targets like reading a certain number of pages by the end of the week.

Local libraries can be a mine of information on what is available in your area, and may also have useful books or booklets on self-study skills. Try keeping a simple diary, not just of events, but also of ideas and personal comments. Practise indexing any collections of things that you have at home: articles, handouts, pamphlets, especially those that might be useful for school use, such as recipes, instructions, games with their rules, or places to visit. Practise writing letters; we have all got out of this habit with the widespread use of telephones.

If you have a real problem with any of the skills (be honest with yourself) you could consider taking a Basic Skills course. These are now on offer at most Adult and Further Education Colleges. They also have courses in academic subjects, and you may wish to enrol for one if you did not get many qualifications at school. Subjects like science or mathematics that seemed daunting at school are easier to tackle in college as an adult: you have more confidence to ask important questions when you do not understand. Or you could learn a language that you could use on holiday. The important thing is to get your brain working and do something for yourself.

Your future

The new National Occupational Standards (LGNTO 2001) for TAs are now published. They are based on the concept of competencies. A competence describes what a person can do to a defined standard. (Some people refer to them as 'can-do' statements.) National standards have been drawn up to describe the job of TAs at two levels. National Vocational Qualifications (NVQs) will be written to these standards. The purpose of standards is to align current and future qualifications for TAs, but they will also prove useful for writing job descriptions and reviewing performance.

Thus TAs can be seen to be **competent,** and this can be recorded. If you are not competent, you can still be trained or helped to be competent. It does not put people in a pass/fail situation.

Competencies

An example:

A competence in preparing a learning environment might be:

- prepare purposeful learning environments
- plan display areas
- arrange accessible resource provision

This might mean in practice:
- the environment should cover, over time, a particular curriculum area
- attention should be given to labelling, colour scheme, access for pupils
- safety implications (not blocking fire doors; suspending displays safely; safe use of all equipment)

What are your competencies?

How do we know that it is happening and how might it be recorded?
- Observation and questioning by mentors and other colleagues
- Evidence in planning
- Photographs, diagrams
- Logging activities and use of environment and any outcomes
- Assignments describing the rationale behind the changes

The national standards have been out for consultation from people working in the field and will be up for revision regularly. As 'first time users' (as most of us will be) we should keep open minds and record our impression of their practical workability as we use them. You might find them lengthy and cumbersome at first, but they improve with familiarity.

TAs in LEAs used to accreditation, and NVQs, will be more familiar with standards and competencies than those new to the field. In future, all existing accreditation for TAs will have to relate to the new standards. These will become the nationally recognised competencies. The concept of levels may help the thorny issue of pay scales.

The principles of the NVQs in Early Years Care and Education (see box) are of interest. They were written for those working with children up to eight years old, but the principles are worth talking through with a colleague.

Principles underlying NVQ in Child Care and Education

The welfare of the child
Keeping children safe
Working in partnership with parents and families
Children's learning and development
Equality of opportunity
Anti-discrimination
Celebrating diversity
Confidentiality
Working with other professionals
The reflective practitioner

The levels used in NVQs also relate to the more academic qualification levels that some of you may be used to:

- Level 1: Basic skills award
- Level 2: 'O' Level/GCSE
- Level 3: 'A' Level
- Level 4: Degree standard
- Level 5: Postgraduate awards

The levels relate to some of the things that TAs do, as the table on page 90 shows. Use the list you made of what you do to check against these ideas. This could form part of your professional development review.

Whatever direction you decide to take, your experience as a TA will be both satisfying and helpful. The profession of TA will soon be one that young people in school will ask about and consider as a career. Make the most of it – enjoy!

Possible levelled competencies for TAs			
Possible level	Competencies expected (Supporting the teacher(s) and personal development)	Experiences typical in school (Supporting the school)	Knowledge and understanding (Supporting the pupil and the curriculum, teaching and learning)
1	Carry out instructions Show common sense Follow child protection guidance Respect confidentiality Understand equal opportunities policies	Domestic chores: paint pots and bookmaking Basic child care: knees and knickers In class: keep children on task, facilitate play activities, repeat instructions of teacher	Understand how the school community works, how to be part of a team Take responsibility for own actions Use equipment safely
2	Able to work under the direction of teacher, with selected children Assist in classroom task set by teacher Take charge of own professional development	Facilitate curriculum delivery, carry out practical tasks, e.g. display Work with groups, interacting where appropriate Aware of variety of resource provision See individual needs are different Facilitate independence and know when to intervene and when to stand back	Undertake child observation Develop a framework of understanding of child development See the relevance of activities to intended learning objectives Start to see theory underpinning practice Support individual children with physical needs and facilitate their learning Attend IEP reviews
3	Able to undertake some self-initiated tasks, especially in private nursery situations, but not take responsibility for children's learning in school Evaluate routines Provide welfare, guidance and support to children	Given a curriculum task, devise games, resources, activities to support learning Participate in planning and assessment activities Provide reports and records under direction of teacher Understand the legislative framework of the education system Know about the Code of Practice	Have an awareness of parts of the NC, e.g. literacy and numeracy, or Early Learning Goals Know about all aspects of child development – physical, emotional, intellectual, spiritual, cultural Support children with particular needs and develop expertise – e.g. autism, dyspraxia, Contribute to IEP reviews Relate to parents
4	Work in partnership with teachers Share in planning and assessment Attend school meetings, contribute to decision making Some qualifications will enable training and management responsibilities	Able to take responsibility, under direction of teacher, for a particular aspect of curriculum development, resource management, or equipment maintenance – e.g. ICT, library, SEN resource area, environmental study area Know of Code of Practice, and own role in its use in school Able to lead a team of other TAs/adults	Able to undertake a lengthy observation of a child, or other study with reflection and assignments Understand some of the requirements of the NC Know about learning objectives and aspects of NC Have some understanding of teaching and learning theory Able to contribute to the formulation of IEPs

Glossary of abbreviations

Abbreviation	Term in full
ALS	Additional Literacy Support
ASE	Association for Science Education
CV	Curriculum Vitae
DES	Department of Education and Science (does not exist now)
DfEE	Department for Education and Employment (now the DfES)
DfES	Department for Education and Skills
EY	Early Years
GCSE	General Certificate of Secondary Education
HMI	Her Majesty's Inspectorate
ICT	Information and Communication Technology
IEP	Individual Education Plan
IiP	Investors in People
INSET	In-service Education for Teachers
IT	Information Technology
LEA	Local Education Authority
LMS	Local Management of Schools
NC	National Curriculum
NCVQ	National Council for Vocational Qualifications (does not exist now)
NVQ	National Vocational Qualification
Ofsted	Office for Standards in Education
PE	Physical Education
PSHE	Personal, Social and Health Education
QCA	Qualifications and Curriculum Authority
RE	Religious Education
SATs	Standardised Assessment Tests (originally Tasks)
SCAA	Schools Curriculum and Assessment Authority
SDP	School Development Plan

SEN	Special Educational Needs
SENCO	Special Educational Needs Coordinator
STA	Specialist Teacher Assistant
TA	Teaching Assistant
TAWG	Teaching Assistant Working Group
TTA	Teacher Training Agency

References and further reading

Abbott, J. (1994) *Learning Makes Sense: Recreating Education for a Changing Future*. Letchworth: Education 2000.

Abbott, J. (1997) 'To be intelligent', *Education 2000 News*.

Adey, P. and Shayer, M. (1994) *Really Raising Standards: Cognitive Intervention and Academic Achievement*. London and New York: Routledge.

Aplin, R. (1998) *Assisting Numeracy*. London: BEAM, The National Numeracy Project and the London Borough of Tower Hamlets.

ASE (1996) *Safeguards in the School Laboratory* (10th edn). Hatfield: Association for Science Education.

ASE (2001) *Be Safe: Health and Safety in Primary School Science and Technology* (3rd edn). Hatfield: Association for Science Education.

DfEE (1998) *The National Literacy Strategy: Framework for Teaching*. London: Department for Education and Employment.

DfEE (1999a) *The National Curriculum: Handbook for Primary Teachers in England, Key Stages 1 and 2*. London: Department for Education and Employment and the Qualifications and Curriculum Authority.

DfEE (1999b) *The National Curriculum: Handbook for Secondary Teachers in England, Key Stages 3 and 4*. London: Department for Education and Employment and the Qualifications and Curriculum Authority.

DfEE (1999c) *The National Numeracy Strategy: Framework for Teaching Mathematics*. London: Department for Education and Employment.

DfEE (1999d) *National Literacy Strategy: Additional Literacy Support (ALS)* [Teaching materials]. London: Department for Education and Employment.

DfEE (2000a) *Teaching Assistant File: Induction Training for Teaching Assistants*. London: Department for Education and Employment.

DfEE (2000b) *Working with Teaching Assistants: A Good Practice Guide*. London: Department for Education and Employment.

DfEE (2000c) *SEN Code of Practice on the identification and assessment of pupils with special educational needs and SEN thresholds: Good practice guidance on identification and provision for pupils with special educational needs*. London: Department for Education and Employment.

DfES (2001) *Teaching Assistant File: Induction Training for Teaching Assistants in Secondary Schools.* London: Department for Education and Skills.

Driver, R. (1983) *The Pupil as Scientist?* Milton Keynes and Philadelphia: Open University Press.

Dunne, R. and Wragg, T. (1994) *Effective Teaching.* London and New York: Routledge.

Fox, G. (1998) *A Handbook for Learning Support Assistants.* London: David Fulton Publishers.

Fox, G. (2001) *Supporting Children with Behaviour Difficulties: A Guide for Assistants in Schools.* London: David Fulton Publishers.

Fox, G. and Halliwell, M. (2000) *Supporting Literacy and Numeracy: A Guide for Learning Support Assistants.* London: David Fulton Publishers.

Freiberg, H. J. and Stein, T. A. (1999) 'Measuring, improving and sustaining healthy learning environments', in Freiberg, H. J. (ed.) *School Climate,* 11–29. London and Philadelphia: Falmer Press.

Gardner, H., Kornhaber, M. L., Warren, K. W. (1996) *Intelligence: Multiple Perspectives.* Fort Worth, Philadelphia, San Diego, New York, Orlando, Austin, San Antonio, Toronto, Montreal, London, Sydney, Tokyo: Harcourt Brace College Publishers.

Harding, J. and Meldon Smith, L. (1996) *How to Make Observations and Assessments,* London: Hodder and Stoughton.

Hook, P. and Vass, A. (2000) *Confident Classroom Leadership.* London: David Fulton Publishers.

Hopkins, D. (1995) *The Nature of Teaching.* A lecture given at a meeting of the Basildon Essex Primary Schools' Improvement-Research Project members, 4 November.

Investors in People and DfEE (2000) *Investors in People in Schools.* London: Investors in People and Department for Education and Employment.

Kyriacou, C. (1986) *Effective Teaching in Schools.* Cheltenham: Stanley Thornes.

Kyriacou, C. (1991) *Essential Teaching Skills.* Cheltenham: Stanley Thornes.

Lazear, D. (1994) *Seven Pathways of Learning: Teaching Students and Parents about Multiple Intelligences.* Arizona: Zephyr Press.

LGNTO (2001) *National Occupational Standards for Teaching Classroom Assistants.* London: Local Government National Training Organisation.

Lorenz, S. (1998) *Effective In-class Support.* London: David Fulton Publishers.

MacGilchrist, B., Myers, K. and Reed, J. (1997) *The Intelligent School.* London: Paul Chapman Publishing.

Northledge, A. (1990) *The Good Study Guide.* Milton Keynes: The Open University.

Nuffield Primary Science (1993) *Materials: Teachers' Guide.* London: Collins Educational.

Ofsted (1999) *Handbook for Inspecting Primary and Nursery Schools.* London: Office for Standards in Education.

Russell, T., Longden, K. and McGuigan, L. (1991) *Materials*. Liverpool: Liverpool University Press.

Sammons, P. (1999) *School Effectiveness: Coming of Age in the Twenty-first Century*. Lisse, The Netherlands: Swets & Zeitlingeer.

Sammons, P., Hillman, J. and Mortimore, P. (1995) *Key Characteristics of Effective Schools*. London: Office for Standards in Education.

Schools Council (1980) *Learning Through Science*. London and Milwaukee: Macdonald Educational.

Smith, A. (1996) *Accelerated Learning in the Classroom*. Trowbridge: Redwood Books.

TAWG (2001) *Minutes of the Eighth Meeting of the Teaching Assistants' Working Group*. London: Department for Education and Employment.

TTA (2000) *Progression to Initial Teacher Training for Teaching Assistants* (Information on training courses – survey). London: Teacher Training Agency.

Watkins, C. and Mortimore, P. (1999) 'Pedagogy: what do we know?' in Mortimore, P. (ed.) *Understanding Pedagogy and Its Impact on Learning*, 1–19. London, Thousand Oaks, New Delhi: Paul Chapman Publishing.

Watkinson, A. (1998) 'Supporting learning and assisting teaching: 1', *National Foundation for Educational Research, Topic*, Spring, 1–6.

Wood, D. (1988) *How Children Think and Learn*. Oxford, UK, and Cambridge, Mass.: Blackwell.

Wragg E. C. (1994) *An Introduction to Classroom Observation*. London and New York: Routledge and the Open University.

Written for teachers

Further reading

These might be on the staffroom shelves: dip into them, do not try to read them from cover to cover!

ASE (1996) *Safeguards in the School Laboratory* (10th edn). Hatfield: Association for Science Education.

ASE (2001) *Be Safe: Health and Safety in Primary School Science and Technology* (3rd edn). Hatfield: Association for Science Education.

Blatchford, P. (1989) *Playtime in the Primary School*. London and New York: Routledge.

Brown, G. and Wragg, E. C. (1993) *Questioning*. London and New York: Routledge.

Dunne, E. and Bennett, N. (1994) *Talking and Learning in Groups*. London and New York: Routledge.

Dunne, R. and Wragg, T. (1994) *Effective Teaching*. London and New York: Routledge.

Hook, P. and Vass, A. (2000) *Confident Classroom Leadership*. London: David Fulton Publishers.

Kyriacou, C. (1986) *Effective Teaching in Schools*. Cheltenham: Stanley Thornes.

Kyriacou, C. (1991) *Essential Teaching Skills*. Cheltenham: Stanley Thornes.

Lazear, D. (1994) *Seven Pathways of Learning: Teaching Students and Parents about Multiple Intelligences*. Arizona: Zephyr Press.

Pollard, A. and Tann, S. (1993) *Reflective Teaching in the Primary School* (2nd edn). London and New York: Cassell Educational, National Primary Centre, The Open University.

Rogers, B. (1990) *You Know the Fair Rule*. Harlow: Longman.

Rogers, B. (1994) *Behaviour Recovery*. Harlow: Longman.

Smith, A. (1996) *Accelerated Learning in the Classroom*. Trowbridge: Redwood Books.

Wragg E. C. (1994) *An Introduction to Classroom Observation*. London and New York: Routledge and the Open University.

Wragg, E. C. and Brown, G. (1993) *Explaining*. London and New York: Routledge.

Written for TAs or nursery nurses

Aplin, R. (1998) *Assisting Numeracy*. London: BEAM, The National Numeracy Project and the London Borough of Tower Hamlets.

Bruce, T. and Meggitt, C. (1996) *Child Care and Education*. London: Hodder and Stoughton.

Clipson-Boyles, S. (1996) *Supporting Language and Literacy*. London: David Fulton Publishers.

DfEE (2000) *Teaching Assistant File: Induction Training for Teaching Assistants*. London: Department for Education and Employment.

Fox, G. (1998) *A Handbook for Learning Support Assistants*. London: David Fulton Publishers.

Fox, G. (2001) *Supporting Children with Behaviour Difficulties: A Guide for Assistants in Schools*. London: David Fulton Publishers.

Fox, G. and Halliwell, M. (2000) *Supporting Literacy and Numeracy: A Guide for Learning Support Assistants*. London: David Fulton Publishers.

Harding, J. and Meldon-Smith, L. (1996) *How to Make Observations and Assessments*. London: Hodder and Stoughton.

Headington, R. (1997) *Supporting Numeracy*. London: David Fulton Publishers.

Montague-Smith, A. and Winstone, L. (1998) *Supporting Science and Technology*. London: David Fulton Publishers.

O' Hagan, M. and Smith, M. (1993) *Special Issues in Child Care*. London: Bailliere Tindall.

For teachers but about TAs

Balshaw, M. (1999) *Help in the Classroom* (2nd edn). London: David Fulton Publishers.

DfEE (2000) *Working with Teaching Assistants: A Good Practice Guide*. London: Department for Education and Employment.

Lorenz, S. (1998) *Effective In-class Support*. London: David Fulton Publishers.

General

Freeman, R. and Meed, J. (1993) *How to Study Effectively*. London: The National Extension College Trust and Collins Educational.

Northledge, A. (1990) *The Good Study Guide*. Milton Keynes: The Open University.

Useful addresses

Confederation of Learning Assistants with Specialist Skills (CLASS)
M. R. Stephenson, 83 Maple Road, Dartford DA1 2QY

Professional Association of Nursery Nurses
(A subsection of the Professional Association of Teachers)
2 St James' Court, Friar Gate, Derby DE1 1BT

UNISON
(The Public Services Union)
1 Mabledon Place, London WC1H 9AJ

Index